Collectors' Guide to Antique American Ceramics

If 500 stoneware pitchers were made at the Bennington potteries in 1848—to vary the old story—then it's a safe bet that 1,000 of them are for sale in antique shops today. The explanation, of course, is that many people believe they can identify unmarked pieces and others make the mistake of taking the word of well-meaning antique dealers who may be no better informed than they are.

To help avoid such embarrassing and expensive miscalculations and to provide a basic guide for the uninformed as well as a reference book for the inveterate collector, here is a survey of American ceramics from Colonial times to the early twentieth century that will appeal to novice and connosseur alike. American ceramics is a relatively new field for collectors and one in which "finds" are still possible at prices a young collector can afford.

is part of a story that will prove rewarding to everyone interested in antiques.

Previous Books by Marvin D. Schwartz:

COLLECTORS' GUIDE TO
ANTIQUE AMERICAN GLASS

Collectors'
Guide to

Rockingham earthenware doorstop, Ohio, about 1850. *The Brooklyn Museum Collection.*

Antique American Ceramics

Ceramics

by Marvin D. Schwartz

1969   Doubleday & Company, Inc., Garden City, New York

138

Library of Congress Catalog Card Number 68–27138
Printed in the United States of America
First Edition

Preface

This book covers the broad subject of American ceramics, putting it into context in the history of American style. It surveys the subject, one of the most exciting of the American decorative arts, for the aspiring collector, for the specialist who wants to know where his favorite pottery fits into the entire story, and for the student of Americana who is interested in all phases of the field. The evolution of American ceramic style is emphasized in this survey of the wares and approaches to the design of these wares, but it touches on the technical developments and the growth of the ceramics industry from the first days of settlement to the beginning of the twentieth century.

No attempt has been made here to chronicle each of the thousands of potters who have contributed to this evolution. Only major figures have been mentioned to give some personality to the story, and their work helps to show how the industry developed and spread across the country from a few centers in the East.

In relating the story of the changes in style and the developments in technique, it is hoped that the beginning collector and the student will learn to understand the medium and its evolution well enough to be able to identify a ware by its appearance rather than by its marks. For the beginning connoisseur of ceramics it is essential that he learn to use his eyes to perceive objects rather than depend upon deciphering marks. Marks cannot be a primary means of identification, for they were easily imitated and faked. Although many pieces were marked, many more missed the imprint from a stamp or an inscription that might serve as a guide to its origin. It is wisest to base attributions first on the appearance of a piece in terms of design and on the body material.

American ceramics might very well illustrate a history of American culture. It reflects the evolution of America. In the days of colonial dependence there was a concentration on producing the essentials for daily living. America soon became a center producing ideas and products that influenced other parts of the world. The story of American ceramics begins with the production of the basic utilitarian wares, but just as the seventeenth-century American towns occasionally produced some poetry, one seventeenth-century effort in ceramics was responsible for the manufacture of delft, a more decorative ware. In the eighteenth century the major part of ceramic production was still restricted to providing necessities, just as the accumulation of wealth was more frequently a preoccupation than was the pursuit of abstract philosophical learning. In ceramics utilitarian wares became more hardy and varied, and there were some efforts at producing porcelain, the most sought-after decorative ware. After the Revolution, when poets and painters began to emerge as a struggling group, a greater variety of decorative ceramics was produced. Just as the American painter or writer was distinctively American even though he received stimulation from the Old World, so was the American ceramicist. After the Civil War the American literature and art were more sophisticated, for the American mastered any field he entered. The parallel may still be drawn between the ceramicist and those in other areas of cultural endeavor.

In relating the history of ceramic design in this country, the basic elements that define the American approach to design are implicitly expressed in this book. This account is directed toward the collector, told from the point of view of the art historian, who uses objects as historical documents rather than as focal points in themselves. It is hoped that the reader will be introduced to the study of the subject in its broadest context and that this book will serve as a springboard for more profound study.

Contents

Introduction

American ceramics are a fascinating field for the collector. Rustic or sophisticated, rough or delicate, and large or small examples are available. The artistic range is broad, although first thoughts on the subject bring to mind simple folk wares, for only rarely were examples made before 1800 more ambitious. Some of the most interesting nineteenth- and twentieth-century typically American designs can be seen in ceramics.

American Wares and Some Antecedents The study of American ceramics is complicated by the fact that ceramic wares have always been imported. Distinguishing the native from the imported product can be confusing at times because both locally made ceramics and imports range from crude utilitarian pots to sophisticated decorative vases. The theory that crude wares were always locally made has been disproved. In the nineteenth century it was easier to sell fine French or German porcelains than American. A report of the 1870s said that American porcelain was described as "imported" by shopkeepers anxious for sales. To discern what is typically American it is necessary to identify the consistent elements in American design.

The study of ceramics must begin with a few basic definitions and an understanding of numerous ceramic bodies, each varying in composition. Most simply defined, ceramics are articles made of clay and baked. The temperature of the baking, which is done in an oven called a kiln, affects the strength of the final product. The higher the temperature, the sturdier the ware. Not all clays can be fired at high temperatures. At the highest temperatures clays must be particularly pure or made of special ingredients.

The development of ceramics may be seen in rapid sequence in American wares. When prehistoric man started to use clay, he first baked it in the sun, and then much later in fire. Clay was a worthwhile material because it was readily available, it could be easily shaped, and it made a good container for liquids. In the simplest wares liquids could be held or transported temporarily but not stored because the contents soaked through eventually. One of the first major improvements was that the body was made impermeable. The other problem was that clay is breakable, and while that still bothers us, there have been a long series of improvements to make the body stronger.

In America ceramic bodies can be divided into four main categories. Ordinary clays may be refined for the simple, functional red earthenware. Very friable but cheap to make, it was often covered with a glaze (a glass surface essentially) to make it impermeable. Americans generally used lead for glazes on earthenware to achieve earthen colors—yellow, brown, or green. A refinement of this was earthenware which was made of purer clays that could be fired at a higher temperature, resulting in a lighter body color. This ware was covered with a tin glaze rather than lead, which made it possible to broaden the range of colors. It was used for delftwares made in Europe in the seventeenth and eighteenth centuries and by Americans for nineteenth-century wares in brown and yellow glazes.

Of course, efforts to improve the earthenware body had been going on long before the New World was settled. The phase of improvements most relevant to American ceramics took place in England in the eighteenth and nineteenth centuries. By the eighteenth century the Staffordshire region was the center of a thriving ceramics industry. Its output included every type of ware. Red earthenware made in Staffordshire in quantity was shipped to far points. Also a significant English export were the so-called delftwares, made in the port towns more than in the pottery towns of Staffordshire. In the course of the eighteenth century higher-fired earthenwares were developed as a poor-man's porcelain. At first the thin body was achieved, but it was necessary to use green, brown, or yellow glazes that were artfully combined to make marbleized or tortoise-shell surfaces, until Josiah Wedgwood perfected the off-white creamware. Relatively inexpensive, the ware achieved popularity quickly. An expensive version was ordered by Queen Charlotte (so that it came to be called queen's ware), and Russia's Catherine the Great ordered a set.

Toward the end of the eighteenth century the Staffordshire potteries made molded decorative pieces (particularly pitchers) in high-fired earthenware as well as in stoneware. Yellow, buff, and brown were popular colors for glazes. Rockingham was the name applied to the brown-glazed examples, presumably because the pottery on the estate of the Marquis of Rockingham had introduced the brown. This body continued to be important throughout the nineteenth century and was made in America as soon as large enough kilns were set up to handle it. Rockingham and yellowware were popular American products, and later other bodies were developed. Earthenwares made with refined clays, almost as thin as porcelain, were made with glazes in a full range of colors. The body (seen if a piece is broken) is white or off-white.

A body called stoneware is produced by increasing the temperature again and employing special clays that are plastic. It can resemble porcelain both in the vitrified state and in finished appearance, or it can be rougher than porcelain, depending on either the clays or the objectives. Stoneware had already been developed for both functional and decorative wares when American potters began making it. Stoneware mugs, tankards, and jugs, which were most often covered with salt glazes, were a popular German export in the seventeenth and eighteenth centuries. Between the 1720s and 1770s a more refined type of stoneware called salt glaze was popular in England as a substitute for porcelain. American potters from the eighteenth century on made utilitarian stoneware which was generally salt-glazed and a bluish gray—but the color varied depending on the clays used. Porcelain, the hardest and finest ceramic body, is made with the rarest clays (a combination of feldspar and kaolin) at the highest temperature. The technique of porcelain making had been known as early as the ninth century A.D. in China, but it was 1713 before Europeans discovered the technique.

Experiments led to the discovery of artificial porcelain. It looked like the real thing but was not as hard because it was not fired at as high a temperature. Between the fifteenth and nineteenth centuries there were a number of artificial porcelains, mostly made with glass or the ingredients of glass.

Bone ash was used, particularly in England, for other artificial porcelain bodies. True porcelain was harder and whiter, but the glossier and fuzzier appearance of the artificial (known better as soft paste) appealed to some. Americans made soft paste in the eighteenth century and later, real porcelain.

American Styles 1650–1910

Changes in style and fashion in the arts also affected the history of ceramics. Today collectors emphasize some of the least stylish tendencies of the past because they prefer functional pieces made of stoneware and earthenware, but the art styles of any period should be considered as a framework for any objects studied.

The so-called pilgrim style in America is characterized by three tendencies. Functionalism, a major element of the traditional attitude that began in the Middle Ages, was one. It persisted in middle-class objects and buildings even when fashion affected the decorative arts. A second conservative tendency was the Renaissance influence, which employed classical motifs in symmetrical designs. More advanced was the third phase, the still contemporary baroque style, which was typified by newly invented variations on classical themes in designs that most often were made dramatic by the spacing of parts and the use of color contrasts. All three tendencies were of some importance and are reflected in ceramics.

Designs of seventeenth-century ceramic wares made by Americans were characteristically heavy and bold. Some forms and surfaces are hard to date because craftsmen worked in a timeless tradition. Other forms combined classical and oriental concepts typical of the seventeenth century. Because American wares were supplemented by imports, oriental porcelain and European delftwares were displayed in affluent American households during the seventeenth century.

At the end of the seventeenth century there was the beginning of a new style on the American scene, but it is hardly perceptible in ceramics. The William and Mary style, as it was called, dating 1690–1725 was an American version of the baroque. It was chiefly evident in architecture, painting, and in furniture and silver. Elements of a new style had appeared earlier, but by the end of the seventeenth century, interiors of buildings became grander, with paneling divided into sections in imitation of classical cut-stone or marble designs. There was a more consistent use of elegant furnishings and objects. Decorative ceramic pieces were oriental porcelain or delft, but the more functional earthenware and stoneware were less affected by fashion.

About 1725 there was a radical change in terms of proportions. The new style, called Queen Anne for illogical and complex reasons, is lighter in feeling and more varied than earlier styles. It is a phase of the rococo style that was in fashion on the continent. Basically, it is a combination of classical and oriental motifs, but it is possibly more oriental. The period is one in which a greater interest in people and their comfort is reflected in the decorative arts by the greater variety of forms in every medium. Americans used more Chinese porcelain and delftware. Locally made red earthenware products were produced in quantity. From Staffordshire came a group of harder tablewares that were substitutes for porcelain. These consisted of the molded, white salt-glazed wares, the brown- and tortoise-shell-colored wares popularly called Whieldon, and, after 1760, creamware. Traditional forms were favored for useful red earthenware, but a certain lightness predominant in eighteenth-century decorative arts became a significant characteristic.

After 1750 there was an increase in elegance. Designs often became more elaborate. The name of Thomas Chippendale, a London cabinetmaker whose book of designs published first in 1754 was very influential, has been applied to the style. Chippendale had assembled what was supposedly a compendium of the latest fashions. Elaborately worked decorative furniture is usually associated with him. It was at this time that European porcelain began to be more important, its designs frequently inspired by silver of the day. The American products were decorated with asymmetrical light designs showing oriental influence.

Chippendale was not aware of design innovations that reflected reactions against the rococo, or ignored them and the precise and classical designs of architect Robert Adam. Americans also paid little attention to this new style until the Revolution ended. Then, neoclassicism, sometimes called Hepplewhite or Sheraton after furniture designers whose pattern books illustrated it, became a dominant influence. Designs were more linear, inspired mainly by decorative motifs of Greco-Roman origin. As time went on the influence of ancient classical art was more pronounced, and the forms as well as the decoration imitated it. For sophisticated designs in ceramics Americans favored English creamware and porcelain. The earthenware and stoneware they made subtly reflected the styles of the time but were primarily utilitarian. The post-Revolutionary styles show that designers had become more aware of historical precedents and were seeking new ideas by searching the past. The Empire or Greek Revival style that came into fashion about 1810 was dominant until the 1850s, but sub-styles were introduced after 1830. The rococo, the Gothic, and the Renaissance were among those revived. Each was used to create a suitable setting.

The nineteenth century was a period of extensive diversification in styles. The growth of technology made it possible to increase the types of wares produced. Simple red earthenwares and stonewares were made in rural potteries both for utility and decoration in homes of seemingly styleless country fashion. In the early decades neoclassicism continued to be fashionable, with the bold, heavy designs of the Empire style prevailing. Functional pieces were made of earthenware or stoneware, but the more highly fired earthenware, which had been developed in Staffordshire, was of increasing importance. Americans imported decorative and fashionable creamware and variations of it as well as porcelain. Before 1850 they were able to make the same ceramic bodies as their Old World suppliers.

Ceramics was the medium Americans used first to reflect their interest in earlier historic styles as the basis for new decorative schemes. Both Gothic and rococo revivals were popular from the 1830s through the 1850s. Hunting scenes and floral decorations on the brown-glazed or lighter earthenware pieces demonstrated how the rural taste was satisfied by more ambitious work than red earthenware had offered previously.

The 1860s marked a shift in the approach to design. After copying designs from the past, designers began to attempt to create new forms in which the motifs of the past were employed as they might best complement the basic new functional form. The ideas of the theorist William Morris inspired the new approach. Besides new forms or shapes, however, new sources were tapped and Near or

Middle Eastern design appeared. Design between 1860 and 1890 was primarily eclectic, the whole history of ornament providing the vocabulary for what were hoped to be fresh new concepts. Porcelain manufacturers with pretensions to elegance, as well as artist-craftsmen who were overserious in their determination to revive the crafts, found inspiration in eclecticism. Toward the end of the century the artist-craftsmen became more experimental and sought exotic new sources for ideas. Egyptian ceramics and glass were a source of fresh inspiration, as were Chinese models. Art nouveau, an effort to create a style in the decorative arts that related to painting and sculpture of the time, was taken up by the artist-craftsmen, but most American manufacturers preferred a more precise revival of a range of "traditional" styles. The seventeenth and eighteenth centuries, the basis of designs for nineteenth-century architecture and furniture, were the inspiration for potters, too. The finest work in ceramics, technically speaking, was done at the end of the nineteenth century.

The early twentieth century was a period of technical perfection, but among commercial manufacturers the decorative arts suffered from timidity, avoiding any design innovations.

The emphasis on historical revival modified to suit forms demanded by the circumstances of the time is oftentimes hard to appreciate today. Art nouveau was the source of a lot of work in ceramics which popularized many of its motifs. So the ephemeral maiden of early examples was transformed into the "Gibson Girl." Artist-craftsmen emphasized technical challenges more than design but gradually evolved an aesthetic of importance. The early part of the twentieth century is a period that is hard to evaluate.

This book covers much ground and material that appeals to many tastes in surveying American ceramics. Rather than trying to single out work that is acceptable to followers of any one aesthetic, each period is explained in its context. This survey is a historical analysis rather than a criticism of the field, although it begins with the premise that American craftsmen were particularly able in their approach to design.

CHAPTER I

Advice to the Wary Collector

Faking is a lazy man's road to wealth. The best way for a collector to combat the practice is by learning as much about the subject of his interest as is possible and by relying on his own abilities to determine the quality of the pieces he owns. If you cannot tell the difference between a modern reproduction and an eighteenth-century plate, it is wisest to pay no more than the going rate for the reproduction of anything you buy. If you don't know the difference between a nineteenth-century Hungarian peasant plate and a Pennsylvania German example, it is best to pay only what the former is worth. If that policy had been followed by all collectors, the job of some fakers would have been made much more difficult. There are amazing coincidences in workmanship between nineteenth- and twentieth-century earthenwares made in Tyrolean villages and the wares made by Pennsylvania German potters, but there are cynics who attribute that similarity to the fact that some of the early dealers, who were getting high prices for their Pennsylvania German wares, had migrated from outlying sections of Austria and Hungary and were able to fill in occasional gaps with merchandise from their home towns.

Although there are many temptations to cheat, most dealers are not in business to fool customers. Rather than a ring of Mafia-type operators, undependable dealers are more frequently simply overage dropouts who have not done their homework.

To avoid confusion and to better understand the evolution of material it is a good idea to visit collections that are documented in museums and historical societies in larger cities all over the country. The Henry Ford Museum in Dearborn, Michigan, the Brooklyn Museum, the Metropolitan Museum of Art, and the Smithsonian Institution have the largest collections and should be on the itinerary of any serious student. Making a list of wares that seem interesting and checking on them wherever possible would be logical first steps for an aspiring collector who wants to restrict his early errors.

The study of American ceramics is virgin territory, with several exceptions. Bennington, Pennsylvania German earthenware, and early porcelain are natural areas of overoptimistic attributions because they are expensive fields. Later wares have not been of too much interest to collectors, although interest has begun to rise, along with the prices. There is still no premium price on a good many of the post-Civil War American wares. In these fields then, there is a comfortable margin for error and thus less pressure to learn quickly. It is also an area in which the beginning collector can mature with the field. He can acquire good pieces easily at no great cost, eliminating as he learns to be more discriminating, and not run great risks. But it has the disadvantage of being an area that is less appealing aesthetically.

For those who like to live dangerously but with more handsome possessions, it is wisest to avoid bargains. It is also safest to be very trite in early acquisitions. Buy expensively but only when those pieces which have been published or can be seen in books and museums are available. Following the attributions of the most reputable dealer may be foolhardy if they cannot be substantiated in marked pieces. The dealer may have the knowledge to defend an off-beat attribution, but the beginning collector does not, nor can he, fully understand the reasons for that attribution. Many pieces were never marked. Making attributions is often relatively simple for the knowledgeable collector in the case of some unmarked works, but there are many more that cannot be securely pigeonholed. Some authentic material may not cost as much as known wares. The important safeguard is to avoid paying for Bennington when acquiring a lesser, later New Jersey example.

Knowledge about American ceramics is, of course, the best way to avoid being duped in the market place. Besides firsthand study of pieces in good collections, it is wise to read a few of the basic books. The first and oldest is Edwin Atlee Barber's *The Pottery and Porcelain of the United States* (New York, 1901). Barber was a pioneer in the study of ceramics. His history is an account of the industry that traces it from the beginning to his own time. He also published a book of marks that was surprisingly complete up to the time it was published in 1904. In 1939 and 1947, John Ramsay published a broad treatment of the subject, *American Potters and Pottery,* which also lists potters and their marks. A model book for information on specific areas is *Early New England Potters and Their Wares,* by Lura Woodside Watkins (Harvard University Press, Cambridge, Massachusetts, 1950). It relates the history of ceramic making in the region with care and completeness. There are innumerable articles in *Antiques* magazine. This publication is indexed and available in most libraries. The more adventuresome collector will encounter the difficulty that the more recent periods have not been studied. Accounts of them, if they exist at all, will be in the trade journals of the time. These are hard to find outside of major libraries in the larger cities.

A seasoned collector will always confess that he has made mistakes. But often overconfidence will conceal from him the realization that he is becoming slipshod in his connoisseurship. Ideally the beginning collector should probably never step beyond the limits of his knowledge, but perhaps it is more fun to make mistakes and learn from them.

CHAPTER II

Earthenware

A *Simple* *Definition*

Red earthenware is one of the easiest things to make in a kiln. It can be made of almost any kind of clay fired at a relatively low temperature. Americans produced it when they first settled, and it continued to be a significant product until the close of the nineteenth century, utilizing local clays in kilns that were fairly easy to set up.

For red earthenware, clay was minimally purified by milling or grinding out only the largest rocks and dirt. The wet, clean clay was made into a shape by the potter manipulating gobs of it on a simple potter's wheel. As the clay was spun around, the potter shaped it. The clay body would be permeable if it was not glazed, so that in most instances a lead glaze was applied by the American craftsman, with a resulting green-, brown-, or yellow-colored surface.

Decoration consisted of patterns incised on the outer surface, or stripes of light cream color, called slip, and a light clay applied to surfaces in a heavy liquid form. Earthenware is the ceramic body that is used most commonly. It varies in hardness depending upon the nature and purity of the clay and the temperature at which it was fired. As the

1. Brown-glazed earthen-ware chamber-pot fragment, Massachusetts, about 1740. *The Brooklyn Museum Collection, lent by courtesy of the Smithsonian Institution.*

temperature rises, the unglazed body lightens in color and becomes harder. Incised decoration is popularly known as "sgraffito," the Italian word for scratch, because in the late nineteenth century when histories were first written, Italian pottery was studied enthusiastically.

Functional Wares 1650–1900

Americans produced red earthenware that was primarily functional, with designs forthright and bold. The earliest American products are difficult to distinguish because in the seventeenth century not all simple wares were made locally. English potters made simple wares for export which have turned up at seventeenth-century sites in several American colonies. These are a little harder than the usual American products so that the body is a lighter color than the typical American examples. According to research by Malcolm Watkins, a Smithsonian Institution curator, the potteries of North Devon made these wares which had been mistaken for

American earthenware products because it seemed logical that simple earthenwares were made locally. The North Devon product is characteristically yellow-glazed and decorated with incised floral and leaf ornament and was made in quantity for export. The history of seventeenth-century American ceramics may be gleaned from a variety of documents, but very few examples actually survive. The distinguishing characteristics of the work of American potters are difficult to enumerate under the circumstances. Early records mention potters in every colony, but finding their output is another problem. Excavations at Jamestown, Virginia, turned up a quantity of pottery which is now identified as European. The New York potters are identified in records and their locations have been determined, but no clearly documented material is known. Probably the potters who are listed supplied simple ceramics. Apparently bricks were made locally so that there were kilns in operation. With the evidence on hand, it is impossible to be sure of the nature of the ceramics made there.

New England sites have yielded more early material, so to some degree, they can be used as an

2. Earthenware bowl, brown glaze with slip decoration, Massachusetts, about 1740. *The Brooklyn Museum Collection, lent by courtesy of the Smithsonian Institution.*

index of what was general. The regional aspects of local American design would not be considered, but there is little reason to believe that functional wares were decorative enough to reflect subtleties of American style. With the information and documentation on hand it would appear that there was no exceptional ceramic manufacture in any one of the American colonies in the seventeenth century.

Basic pottery shapes remained conservative enough to resemble medieval prototypes from the seventeenth century until almost the middle of the eighteenth century. Forms such as a globular jug with a high cylindrical neck were used over a long period and not abandoned before the later eighteenth century. Handled jars with short necks, rather like vases, repeated classical shapes. The form had been used always, so that the New England potter was simply following a tradition. By the end of the eighteenth century this shape was becoming more popular for stoneware than earthenware, however. Red-earthenware potters varied in their output, but they generally concentrated on useful forms that

3. Earthenware jar with cover, Portland Pottery, Maine, early nineteenth century. *The Metropolitan Museum of Art, The Rogers Fund, 1918.*

could be made on the potter's wheel. Sale lists of
early makers included platters, pots, jugs, and many
other containers. There is evidence that teapots were
made in the eighteenth century in the South and
in New England. The criteria for establishing an
early dating (which means before the Revolution)
is that the shapes be simple, turned on a wheel,
and easily made. Decoration, both incised and slip,
was applied to popular pieces from time to time.
Among pieces likely to turn up are mugs, jars, and
pots in warm brown and green glazes. The mugs
are cylindrical with plain, curving handles. Teapots
are squat and glazed in various kinds of brown.

The shapes of red earthenwares began to reflect
changes in technique and fashion in about 1800.
The small potters introduced short-cut techniques
to speed up their production, so that molds were
introduced for some pieces that had earlier been
made more simply on the potter's wheel. Improvements in transportation made it possible for even
the smaller potters to be more selective in choos-
ing clays. By using purer ingredients, they were able
to work more easily and to produce more varied
objects. The more highly fired and vitreous stoneware replaced red earthenware, restricting the more
porous ware to the kitchen and dairy, where in-

4. Brown-glazed earthenware mug,
late eighteenth century. *The Metropolitan Museum of Art, The
Rogers Fund, 1912.*

expensive objects were needed in rural or simple households. Red earthenware continued to be important for pieces that had to be made as inexpensively as possible. It was the specialty of small rural potters in the nineteenth century, but it was also made in larger city potteries. In the early 1800s Philadelphia was one center where a number of potters were reported to be producing a variety of wares. The advertisements of potters there and in other metropolitan centers show that redware was produced along with creamware and stoneware.

The repertory of redware forms grew limited as time went on. Having made everything out of red earthenware in the early years, potters restricted its use as they broadened their output. It was best for inexpensive wares in shapes as simple as possible. Often the use of a mold resulted in a seam on the side of some pieces. The glazes appeared to be less casually applied, and black came to be used along with the browns and greens. In studying the wares, another factor to be remembered is that the American wares were used in conjunction with imported wares. Gradually, Staffordshire began providing hardier functional wares inexpensively enough to compete with the native red earthenwares. This trend began at the end of the eighteenth century, and as economic conditions improved for Americans, finer imported wares replaced crude local products even on the tables of unpretentious homes.

One group of standard products that are known to be very early persisted until the last of the potters stopped working at the beginning of the nineteenth century. These included jugs with narrow openings topping almost globular bodies. Early examples are exceedingly rare, possibly because imports were so popular. The more squat or nearly globular they

were, the later the form. Brown, green, and yellow glazes were used over a long period, but black is more frequently encountered on late examples.

The pie plate, with its notched lip enclosing a brown-glazed interior, is more often late than early. Brown and black glazes on the inside are often lightened by the slip decoration in simple wavy-line patterns or by an occasional inscription which suggests that caution is needed in dating. One reading

5. Earthenware mug, New England, 1820–60. *The Brooklyn Museum Collection.*

6. Earthenware mug, 1840–90. *The Brooklyn Museum Collection.*

7. Earthenware milk pitcher, 1850–90. *The Brooklyn Museum Collection.*

8. Plate made at Singer Pottery, Bucks County, Pennsylvania, 1810. *The Brooklyn Museum Collection, lent by Huldah Cail Lorimer.*

"Happy New Year 1889" appears to be as old and worn as any that have survived. Platters of a variety of sizes, flat-bottomed with out-flaring sides (possibly more aptly called deep dishes), were used for cooking and as milk pans. The sides were too shallow for some uses and relatively high for others, and in many early examples (1760–1800) the glaze was on the inside only. Pots, deeper containers, with sides almost straight and proportionately high in relation to the diameter of the base, were popular until the end of the nineteenth century. Their simplicity makes it almost impossible to date by shape. Small covered pots with curving sides were used in New England in the nineteenth century. That famous form, the bean pot, was introduced in the 1840s as an earthenware form but soon was made of stoneware. Bean pots were originally inexpensive and, therefore, easily expendable. The jugs were made for beverages that alleviated toothaches but sometimes upset the balance of the imbiber. Milk pans and bowls began to be made in harder bodies, too.

Decorative
1730–1860
The Emphasis
on Pennsylvania

Decorative red earthenwares form a special category. Almost all seem to be attributed to one area, Pennsylvania, because the first sgraffito wares recognized as American were discovered there. Actually there is no particular logic in thinking that wares with sgraffito and pictorial slip decoration were made exclusively in Pennsylvania. The decoration is a type that was known all over Europe and, to a lesser degree, in England. Essentially a "peasant ware," eighteenth-century sgraffito and slip-decorated pottery is derived from an earlier decorative ware developed in Italy in the Renaissance—majolica. The production of decorative ceramics in Europe was revived in the late fourteenth and early fifteenth centuries, when most ceramics for display were imported from Spain but came to Italy by way of the island of Majorca. The name majolica, a corruption of the island's name, was applied to it.

Decorative motifs on the ware were a combination of Near Eastern and classical inspirations. Although majolica is a higher-fired earthenware covered with a tin-oxide glaze, it was no problem to render it in lead glazes, which limited the range of color. In the popular version, identified most readily as a peasant ware, the decoration was gradually limited, avoiding obvious classical themes and concentrating on motifs most easily recognized by people without education. Flowers abounded, but symbols also came in, so that the repertory included the double-headed eagle, the pelican biting its breast, and men on horseback who generally were supposed

9. Earthenware dish, Pennsylvania, about 1800. *The Brooklyn Museum Collection, lent by Huldah Cail Lorimer.*

10. Earthenware pie plate, Pennsylvania, about 1800. *The Brooklyn Museum Collection.*

11. Earthenware pie plate by Johannes Leman, Montgomery County, Pennsylvania, about 1830. *The Brooklyn Museum Collection, lent by Huldah Cail Lorimer.*

12. Earthenware bowl, Pennsylvania, 1775. *The Brooklyn Museum Collection, lent by Huldah Cail Lorimer.*

to represent heroes of the moment. The urn of flowers and the tulip were both popular eighteenth-century decorative subjects, and there is some feeling that conceivably their popularity rested on the fact that both can be traced to seventeenth-century imagery, in which they were used to symbolize the tree of life and the bleeding heart of Jesus. The connection is apt if there was any way of proving that the images were a part of the visual language of the eighteenth century. All of the decorative schemes were used on both American and European examples. Slip and scratch were used for both wares, too, so that caution must be exercised in making attributions.

The group of popular types is surprisingly consistent in the simple direct approach to decoration. There is a certain variety in the color of the unglazed parts of a piece of sgraffito or slipware. Generally speaking, American examples are darker and brownish red, while European examples tend to be lighter. Because the color is determined by the heat of the kiln and the mixture of clays, it was not possible to adhere to rigid rules.

For the beginning collector and the man who wants to be sure he has acquired what will never be questioned, it is safest to buy only close variations of carefully documented examples. Certainly there is a fine group of consistent work to be called American, or Pennsylvanian. Until the more questionable examples can be traced back to the pottery where they were made, it is not accurate to make attributions.

Today, it is generally assumed that all scratch wares were made in Pennsylvania. Examples found in Pennsylvania are called local (even if lost only days before). Those pieces found in other parts of the country are thought to have been brought there

13. Earthenware pie plate by Samuel Troxel, Montgomery County, Pennsylvania, about 1840. *The Metropolitan Museum of Art, gift of Mrs. Robert W. de Forest, 1933.*

by people moving from Pennsylvania. Most amazing is the fact that the attribution to Pennsylvania was first made in 1891. In that year Edwin Atlee Barber, while studying a piece he regarded as German, found an inscription that was peculiarly Pennsylvanian. The last potteries had just been closed, but nobody knew what they had made! After Barber chanced upon his discovery, he began collecting the work he regarded as Pennsylvania-made and learned about a number of potters who had concentrated on its production. The basis of his research was logical, but it seems impossible to be sure that other areas did not produce the scratch wares, too.

Dr. Barber inspired a number of collectors to concentrate on decorated earthenwares, so that by the 1920s it was the most eagerly sought American ware. Once the high prices were established, no matter where an example turned up, it was called Pennsylvanian. Since members of families that sell inherited possessions rarely want anyone to know, histories are frequently lost. One obviously Pennsylvania German group has German inscriptions that have peculiarly Pennsylvanian idioms. These were used as the key to a type of ware that has been limited in origin, but the basic elements of style, such as the combination of slip and the incised linear decoration, need not have been exclusive.

The scratch-ware technique of decoration was popular in the English potteries, too. The yellow-glazed ware exported to the colonies was in the same tradition as the Pennsylvania examples and conceivably could have been made anywhere that the potters went. The Pennsylvania German wares (to keep the popular name) were made as decorative pieces to be used in simple homes. They consisted of plates and jars in particular, but these were also more complex jugs, sugar bowls, and toys. The motifs used were generally limited to flowers, birds, and animals, which seem to be traditional ceramic subjects, and to human figures, which are more likely derived from prints of the time.

14. Earthenware sugar bowl by Johannes Leman, Montgomery County, Pennsylvania, about 1830. *The Brooklyn Museum Collection.*

15. Earthenware jelly mold, Pennsylvania, nineteenth century. *The Brooklyn Museum Collection.*

16. Earthenware flower holder, Pennsylvania, about 1860. *The Brooklyn Museum Collection, lent by Huldah Cail Lorimer.*

Two techniques of decorating, by scratching the surface or by drawing in slip, were used at the same time. Slip was used also for much simpler decoration on predominantly functional wares made at many potteries. For scratch or sgraffito the entire surface is covered with slip—a light liquid clay. It is applied to the form after it has hardened but before firing—and the linear motifs are scratched through the slip. Often the slip has other colors added onto the surface that look as though they were sponged on. The designs scratched in are simple linear patterns that vary in craftsmanship. The figures are sometimes artfully rendered; other times the rendering is clumsy, almost childlike in ignoring elements of form. One of the more confusing aspects of connoisseurship in this field is that late eighteenth-century and nineteenth-century craftsmen often were clumsy in executing detail, so that a genuine piece can look as bad as if made by the unsure hand of a faker.

The basic research on the Pennsylvania German potters has not been carried very far since the beginning of the century. Then, fewer than fifty craftsmen were identified, and groups of work were attributed to individual potters who had signed key pieces. Their potteries were centered in Montgomery and Bucks counties, near deposits of good clay. Most of their names are German and may be traced to Palatinian or Swiss families, but there is an English name in the group. The activity was greatest after the Revolution until the middle of the nineteenth century, although one example dated 1733 was reported, and a few examples dating from close to the end of the nineteenth century demonstrate that traditional forms, like old soldiers, never die.

One of the earliest potters about whom anything is known established his pottery in about 1763, at

Wrightstown, Bucks County, Pennsylvania. He was
Joseph Smith, a man of English origin, born in
1721, who was still working in 1799. There are floral
and bird designs on pie plates attributed to him,
but more unusual are the tea caddies. One, dated
1767, has a sketchy rendition of a tree with birds
flanking it. The caddy or canister was fashionable
tea equipage in 1767, known better in English and
European porcelain than in simple earthenware.
Smith obviously derived his inspiration for both the
form and decoration from elegant Old World versions. The existence of a tea caddy by Smith makes
one wonder if he did more examples that were
based on sophisticated wares. He seems to have
made the caddy for a daughter, Esther, whose name
is inscribed on it, so that it probably was done as
a kind of tribute to show paternal devotion as much
as his potter's skill. Smith pieces have inscriptions
in English which occasionally are in the spirit of the
homey German examples, and add substance to the
theory of some students that sgraffito is not a purely
German phenomenon. One of Dr. Barber's favorite little poems came from a piece that has now
disappeared:

> Here is health to the man who has
>   a half Joe
> And has the heart to lend it;
> Let the dogs take him who has
>   a whole Joe
> And hasn't the heart to spend it.

Operation of the Smith pottery was continued in
the nineteenth century by Thomas Smith, probably
Joseph's son.

A potter of German origin working in Montgomery County (the exact site is not known),
George Huebener, was active between about 1785
and 1800. He used bird and flower designs that

are easily associated with German models. The double-headed eagle was one motif he favored. It was a Hapsburg symbol which Pennsylvanians simplified and pacified. Huebener's inscriptions were often in two circles and offered advice:

> Die Schussel ist von Ert gemacht
> Wann sie verbricht der Hafner lacht
> Darun neempt sie in acht.

> (The dish is made of earth
> When it breaks the potter laughs
> Therefore take care of it.)

Huebener's work was most often marked only with initials.

Another potter working in Montgomery County, John Leidy, whose dated work is from the 1790s and early 1800s, chose occasionally caustic German sayings like:

> Wer etwas will verschwiegen haben
> Der derf es seiner frau nicht sagen.

> (He who would have something secret
> Dare not tell it to his wife.)

Leidy was born in 1780 and died in 1838 but concentrated on the tanning business in the later years of his life. He used slip decoration on a dark ground in some of his work. Tulips were a favored motif.

One of the more important potters of the early nineteenth century, David Spinner of Bucks County, found inspiration for decoration in contemporary narrative subjects—or at least figures. Two signed examples show men on horseback racing; another marked "Lady Okie" shows a lady on horseback. Spinner incised amusing but clumsy designs. He used figures in eighteenth-century dress, outmoded some thirty years, so that it would seem

17. Earthenware pie plate by David Spinner, Bucks County, Pennsylvania, about 1800. *The Brooklyn Museum Collection.*

that prints could have served as a source of inspiration.

The same spirit and same old-fashioned element is found in work by Johannes Neesz, a potter in Montgomery County who was born in 1775 and died in 1867. A subject for which Neesz was famous was the man with sword and horn on horseback in Continental Army uniform. It has been interpreted as a representation of George Washington. The inscriptions do not substantiate the interpretation:

> Ich bin geritten uber berg und dahl
> Nab metger funtenuber all.

> (I've ridden over hill and dale
> And found girls everywhere.)

But there are other claims made in the inscriptions, such as the plaintive comment of the lack of girls and, more attuned to the political situation, the observation that disloyalty is everywhere.

18. Earthenware monkey and dog, attributed to Haig Pottery, Philadelphia, about 1840. *The Brooklyn Museum Collection.*

19. Earthenware flower holder by Charles Headman, Bucks County, Pennsylvania, 1849. *The Brooklyn Museum Collection.*

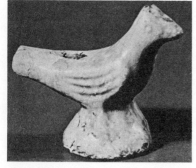

20. Earthenware whistle in the form of a bird, Pennsylvania, 1840–60. *The Brooklyn Museum Collection.*

21. Earthenware bank by Elizabeth D. Herr, Philadelphia, about 1860. *The Brooklyn Museum Collection, lent by Huldah Cail Lorimer.*

Neesz' son, John Nase, was his successor, carrying on his rich tradition and what must have been a flourishing business. Nase worked in scratch and slip decoration, doing plates with the full range of motifs and more unusual forms, such as a sugar bowl with black ground and slip ornament of a form with fairly elaborate cover. The later wares, made from the 1830s on, often have a black-glaze ground that was used on the continent over a long period. Hungarian examples of the early twentieth century may be confusingly close in spirit to the work of Nase.

Toys and miniatures are a category that must have been popular in the nineteenth-century earthenware potteries. Amusing animals, glazed in the warm brown of functional wares, have folk-art qualities most characteristic of mid-nineteenth century expression. Since the techniques for the realistic rendering of hair and other details would seem to be influenced by the poodles, popular in higher-fired wares of the middle of the century and later, it is tempting to date most miniature animals after 1850. Horses, birds, monkeys, and bears were included in the repertory. Whistles were often made in the shape of birds—but modern Mexican exam-

22. Black-glazed earthenware teapot by John Mann, Rahway, New Jersey, 1857. *The Brooklyn Museum Collection.*

23. Black-glazed earthenware coffeepot, attributed to Thomas Haig, Philadelphia, about 1825. *The Metropolitan Museum of Art, The Rogers Fund, 1922.*

ples cause confusion for some collectors who act hastily. A favored form of earthenware bank was the Empire chest of drawers made in a mold and more likely the product of the larger urban pottery rather than individual craftsmen.

Ornamented red earthenwares have been mainly attributed to Pennsylvania. The ware is in a tradition that includes both English and continental areas, but the Middle European peasant centers continued the tradition until the end of the nineteenth century, as did the rural Pennsylvanians. In working out attributions, it is important to realize that the technique was popular over a wide area for a long time. The securely documented wares are fairly limited to earthen colors glazed on a body fired at a relatively low temperature. Designs also come within a narrow range and reflect the American taste for directness and simplicity. An economy of line and an avoidance of elaboration that could not be handled well are evident. In spite of occasional clumsy figures, American craftsmen were consistent in their ability to select and apply what was good from fashionable models, without being overwhelmed as were provincial Europeans.

For the collector, before getting fired with enthusiasm for any of the earthenware types, a study of the attributed examples at one of the major museums, such as the Philadelphia Museum of Art, the Metropolitan Museum of Art, or the Brooklyn Museum, should be undertaken.

CHAPTER III

Stoneware

A Simple Definition

Stoneware is most familiar on the American scene as the large grayish-colored functional ware. Used for jars and jugs, it has to be made from special clays—often bluish—that can take the intense heat required to make the ware. Most often stoneware has an orange-rind surface, which is a result of the glaze made of common salt thrown into the kiln during the firing. The body is practical because it is nearly impervious to water and acids. It is an ideal container for liquids.

The Introduction of the Ware in Sixteenth-Century Germany

The ware was known first in the Rhineland, where it was developed before 1500. Used for jugs and tankards, the decoration consisted of relief patterns, often Renaissance in origin. One popular motif for simpler jugs was a bearded head placed on the neck. These have been variously called "Bartman," graybeard, and bellarmine. The ware was used for ambitious, elaborate works in the sixteenth century but for more and more functional examples by the eighteenth century.

Stoneware is almost as hard as porcelain, and refined versions were used as a substitute for it in the eighteenth century, especially one called salt glaze. English potters employed it for fine wares such as Wedgwood's Jasper (famous as the pale blue and white decorative body).

The
Eighteenth-
Century Types

The precise beginning of stoneware production on the American scene is difficult to document. Evidently Americans did not make it before the eighteenth century. Finding the proper clays and building large kilns were difficulties Americans did not cope with earlier. American clays that were right for stoneware were first found in New Jersey and Staten Island. Probably the earliest American stoneware was made there. Unfortunately, the few pieces inscribed with early dates have no marks to show where they were made, nor is there any way to confirm these dates as the date of manufacture. One piece, marked 1722, is too simple to attribute to any specific place. It might have been an import. Because there is no proof that there was an American kiln large enough to make it at that time, it is best not to accept it as American until further evidence of early stoneware is uncovered.

American stoneware of the early period needs further research, but there were American potters producing significant stoneware before 1750. So far, the site that has been excavated with the most revealing results is that at Yorktown, Virginia, where Ivor Noel Hume and Malcolm Watkins have discovered fragments and documents to show that a fine potter was active there. His name was William Rogers, and he died in 1739, leaving an inventory which included stoneware bottles and fragments. Rogers produced a great variety of forms. Excavations have uncovered mugs, jugs, and bowls that are close to so-called Fulham ware. This is a thin, salt-glazed stoneware that is often partly brown in color and was attributed to Fulham but was often made in London. The fact that this was made at Yorktown makes it seem possible that there were other early potteries producing stoneware in the American colonies by about 1730.

In the 1730s, according to one nineteenth-century tradition, a stoneware kiln was being operated on Manhattan Island. Historians have tended to question the tradition, although there is no reason why stoneware could not have been attempted then. Manhattan was a relatively short distance from sources of proper stoneware clay.

Another American stoneware pottery operating as early as 1730 is documented by records in Philadelphia, where Anthony Duché had applied for a subsidy and monopoly to manufacture stoneware. Duché's interests were reflected in the work of his sons. One of them, Andrew, went to Savannah, where he tried to establish a porcelain factory. Another son, James, was brought to Boston in 1742 to assist Isaac Parker, a potter who wanted to learn how to make stoneware. Parker also tried to get assistance from the legislature and received a loan in 1742, just before he died. His widow, Grace, carried on in partnership with Thomas Symmes. *The Boston Gazette*, April 16, 1745, carried an advertisement in which Symmes offered "blue and white stoneware of forty different sorts . . ."

So few of the early wares have been discovered that earlier writers such as Arthur Clement failed to mention them. Stonewares made before 1750 may be easier to identify when more is known about them. Archeologists have yet to investigate all the areas where stoneware may turn up. Once the basic types are understood, collectors will be making discoveries of early stoneware, a field of study that is now neglected.

24. Advertisement from Norwich, Connecticut, late eighteenth century. *The Metropolitan Museum of Art, The Rogers Fund, 1918.*

25. Stoneware jug by John Crolius, New York, 1775. *The Metropolitan Museum of Art, The Rogers Fund, 1934.*

Potteries producing stoneware at the time of the Revolution are better known. There have been some excavations at a few of the New Jersey sites that have uncovered fragments of the heavy utilitarian wares with dates as early as 1775. Unfortunately, this pioneer work was undertaken by enthusiasts who had no archeological training. They unearthed only what they wanted, fragments that matched examples in their collections.

One key site for information on the manufacture of stoneware has been that of the Morgan pottery in Cheesequake, now a part of Madison, New Jersey. There, James Morgan, working from about 1775 to 1785, made stoneware. A part of one jar bears the 1775 date. Other pieces have blue decoration over inscribed patterns in designs close to examples that continued to be made into the nineteenth century.

The Cheesequake fragments suggest a limited range of stoneware products. The factory made mugs, bowls, and plates, as well as jugs and jars. The forms were simple, but decoration was varied. Mugs from this site have geometric designs inscribed on the front and are colored with blue enamel. Spiral motifs were applied in bands of blue around some pieces. Blue was the usual color for decorating stoneware. Generally designs were incised, and the color was added for emphasis. Cheesequake examples are plainer and more boldly designed than the English imports excavated at Williamsburg. They seem to be heavier and inspired by later wares than the Yorktown examples.

The large jugs, jars, and pots that were made at Cheesequake in the 1770s are typical of the work of many potteries of the time. Forms were simple and like much earlier (and later) European rural wares of lower-fired clays. There were details such as handles modeled by hand to give the pieces a less mechanical appearance. At their best the American examples are a combination of traditional primitivism and a functionalism that kept them simple, bold, and easier to date than later rural wares by Italian or Mexican village potters.

The New York wares contemporary to the examples dug up at Cheesequake are closely related in appearance. Probably many examples would be impossible to attribute specifically. There are, however, some marked pieces. Crolius of Manhattan is identified as the maker who marked his work I.C. It was made before 1790. John Remmey II, active 1762 to 1793, also initialed examples of his work. His pottery is recorded as being close to the one operated by Crolius. Stoneware made before 1800 survived occasionally because it was easier to ignore jars than to destroy them. It had been intended for ordinary utilitarian wares. It was inexpensive enough to be disposed of after a few years. Actually it was less breakable than earthenware and remained in better condition after being used for oil or other heavy liquids. Nonetheless, relatively few examples have survived. The chances of discovering more are limited, although the growing number of aware people serves as assurance that it would be recognized if a cache was uncovered.

The Nineteenth-Century Developments

Stoneware became increasingly popular, and the period between 1800 and 1850 marked the emergence of a widespread stoneware industry. It was the material used for practical functional wares at potteries that were becoming increasingly versatile. Potters were able to make the body that suited the situation and could decide between the cheapest and best. For many, although they could make high-fired earthenwares, they could not compete with

26. Stoneware jug, Norwich, Connecticut, early nineteenth century. *The Metropolitan Museum of Art, The Rogers Fund, 1918.*

English imports, so earthenware and stoneware were the limit. Transportation was good enough by then so that locally made primitive substitutes of fine wares were no longer necessary. This meant that with only a few exceptions simple functional wares were the stoneware products for American potters. The forms that were most common were large jars and jugs—containers for liquids of various sorts. Potteries with large kilns were constructed in many parts of New England and the Middle States, as well as Ohio. Names of many potters have come down, but unless their work is marked, attributions are hard to make because things tend to be similar.

The making of stoneware was a practical business. Forms were determined by needs and not by a potter's desire to be inventive, so that at first earthenware forms were adapted to stoneware. Hence changes were the result of conforming to the needs of modifications of the manufacturing processes. Stoneware was used in general for plain functional wares in the middle of the nineteenth century, but there were exceptions. Potteries in remote areas occasionally used stoneware for decorative pieces. Figures inspired by earthenware examples from Staffordshire are encountered from Midwestern sources. The Philadelphia potteries, which produced a variety of wares, also resorted to making inexpensive decorative earthenware banks and figures.

Wherever nineteenth-century stoneware was made, the decoration was either in the neoclassical spirit or a manifestation of folk art. Neoclassical ornament consisted of small-scale stamped or painted patterns, swags, or eagles. The forms were also inspired by the Greco-Roman models when possible, and in the course of time both decoration and shape were made in heavier proportions in conformity to the Empire style. Being sure of period is always a challenge when a piece is not marked, because conservatism was the rule except when technological factors dictated innovations in shape. As time went on, more large potteries were active, making wares that were as simple as possible. These simple shapes were decorated with folk-art motifs. The more popular subjects included animals in rural settings and birds that were incised and colored blue in primitive patterns.

The wide color range of stoneware occurred because the clays varied from one region to another. Seemingly, better materials resulted in lighter-colored bodies, but when far from fine clay deposits, potters tended to stretch their supplies of expensive clays brought from a distance by adding local materials. This made for darker bodies. Buffs and dark browns are encountered particularly in wares from New England and parts of the West. Potters such as Xerxes Price or Warne and Letts, who worked in New Jersey in the Cheesequake area, signed or marked examples that appear to have been made by

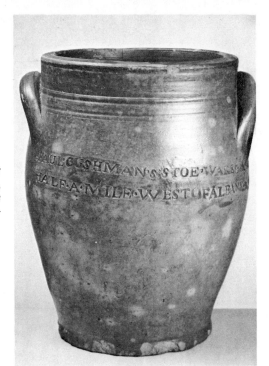

27. Stoneware jar by Paul Cushman, Albany, New York, 1809. *The Brooklyn Museum Collection.*

28. A collection of stoneware from *The Henry Ford Museum, Dearborn, Michigan,* showing variety of forms.

individual craftsmen if the casually fashioned handles of jars and jugs are noticed. Later, pieces were
fashioned more carefully so that they closely resemble each other, as if made by more complex factory
methods.

The early forms were made first in New Jersey
and the surrounding area, but Connecticut, Massachusetts, and Vermont potters were soon producing
related wares. By the early nineteenth century, stoneware was made in Ohio, West Virginia, and western
Pennsylvania, with early forms continuing to be
used. Marked examples can be traced, but it is
difficult to either date or trace those without names.

29. Stoneware jug by
Daniel Goodale, Hartford,
Connecticut, about 1825.
*The Brooklyn Museum
Collection.*

The simple jugs and jars were supplied by the local makers, however, and should be compared with known local products. Many of the designs were determined by the size of the pottery and its techniques of production, so that style is generally a secondary factor.

The Bennington potteries were among the largest suppliers of the typically mass-produced wares. When it was used, folk decoration adds a special charm and makes one forget about problems of the factory. Typical is the deer reclining in a rural setting. Like all folk art, the deer has that quality of seeming unique and the design of a particular in-

30. Stoneware jug by Peter Cross, Hartford, Connecticut, about 1810. *The Brooklyn Museum Collection.*

dividual. Nonetheless, with care and persistence one can acquire ten examples that are very much alike.

Small, practical stoneware flasks without decoration were produced by some of the potteries. Bowls and plates, which were uncovered at Cheesequake, probably were less significant than the plain functional wares. By the middle of the nineteenth century, when other wares were being developed, it would not have been worthwhile making the forms that would be more sensible in Rockingham or the other high-fired earthenwares.

In the Midwest as well as New England, stoneware was occasionally used for decorative pieces. Water coolers were frequently made in stoneware. These tended to follow fashion. Crude versions of

31. Stoneware bowl and pitcher, probably by S. Purdy, Zoar, Ohio, 1840. *The Henry Ford Museum, Dearborn, Michigan.*

neoclassical designs, rustic patterns, and other designs characteristic of the nineteenth-century spirit
are found. In the main these were large and gross
renditions of designs and forms that were known
earlier but were transformed into the Victorian style
by the handling of details.

32. Stoneware pitcher by
John Remmey III, Phila-
delphia, (Working, 1793–
1820). *The Brooklyn Mu-
seum Collection.*

CHAPTER IV

More Ambitious Earthenware and Stoneware

Higher-fired earthenware is the most familiar ceramic body—the one that plastics are replacing. Not as thin or as strong as porcelain, it is a good substitute because it costs less and breaks easily enough so that an earthenware set disappears from the ordinary household before it goes out of style. This type of body is made by using more refined clays that can be fired at a higher temperature to make them harder and thinner. This body is best known to collectors of Americana in a wide variety of nineteenth-century wares, but more must still be learned about the earlier efforts. The body becomes lighter in color as the temperature and ingredients change, so that it has been called yellow-ware by some.

The European Background   In European ceramics, higher-fired earthenware had been introduced centuries earlier, and at the time of the first settlements in America, the more elegant decorative wares were made of it. Delftware is a good example of one popular seventeenth-century earthenware which was made in quantity not only in Delft, but all over Europe. Characteristically delft-wares were covered with a tin glaze which was most often white, and decoration was applied in blue, green, red, and yellow.

33. High-fired earthenware plate, Massachusetts, 1769. *The Brooklyn Museum Collection.*

The primary inspiration for delftware design was the East—both Far and Near—with the relatively thinner models successfully adapted to the thicker occidental ware. Silver was also a source of design; decorative details in relief were derived from it. Delftware was developed as a decorative ware to be used for display pieces, although it was hard enough to serve in the kitchen.

*Early
Developments*

Surprisingly enough, a pottery making delftware was operating by 1685 in the vicinity of Burlington, New Jersey. The ware had become popular both in England and most of northern Europe, and apparently it was functional as well as decorative. It was often referred to as china, and at Burlington the china (Chiney) mentioned in the early records must be delftware. One of the proprietors of the colony of West New Jersey, Daniel Cox, reported in 1689: "I have erected a pottery at Burlington for white and Chiney ware, a great quantity to ye value of £1200 have already made and vended in ye County, neighbor colonies and Islands of Barbados and Jamaica . . ." To confirm interpretations of the term "Chiney ware," commonly encountered in early records as delftware, a piece of a stove tile which survives from this pottery has the delft's typical white glaze. The factory did not last long, and the more ambitious efforts have not been discovered.

American ceramics has been a field of distinctive craftsmanship and design but not of real inventiveness until after 1900. Fashion and its accompanying technological refinements varied first in the Old World, but Americans, as an aware and ever-changing group, made improvements as soon as they could. Skilled craftsmen educated in the New World rarely followed the craft they learned after their apprenticeship, so there was a steady source of new talent and no reason to adhere to old methods of production. The new immigrant brought the latest methods, but in the New World he changed his approach to design and very quickly adopted forms that were more simple and direct. Eighteenth-century American potters learned from English developments how to produce harder wares.

By the middle of the eighteenth century a thin, high-fired earthenware was being produced in England by the large-scale potters in the Staffordshire region as a substitute for porcelain. First they made the multi-colored-glazed Whieldon ware and a short time later the almost-white-glazed creamware. Both were made of nearly white bodies that were fairly thin, and although more breakable than porcelain, they were much less expensive.

American efforts at Whieldon and creamwares are suggested in records, but little evidence has turned up. Again it is likely that it was more commonly made than is documented by examples found so far. Archeologists will have to check the early statements by discovery of examples before we can learn more. Where trained archeologists have worked, the findings are more complete than those spots that have been dug up by men looking solely for material to match what they have collected.

A good example of interesting findings is work to be published by Carolina archeologists. They have been working at a site that once belonged to an operating pottery which produced teapots, bowls, mugs, and a group of forms that are unfamiliar to historians today. The craftsmen were of German origin, and they made what looks like a cross between eighteenth-century Staffordshire and the Pennsylvania wares. When the results of the archeologists can be studied, it should help open a new field for collectors.

A Massachusetts pottery organized about 1769 was ambitious enough to attempt the production of Whieldon. They advertised for apprentices who wanted to learn ". . . the art of making Tortoiseshell Cream and Green Colour Plates, dishes, Coffee and Tea Pots, Cups and Saucers and other articles in the Potter's Business . . ." Their success was boasted about in an almanac the next year. One surviving example of the ware is a bit thicker than typical Whieldon and appears to have been made by making a mold from an English example. Conceivably there are more examples yet to be found. The one surviving piece came down in a family that knew its history.

The failure of enterprises designed to produce luxuries such as fine ceramics was a common occurrence in colonial America. Labor was hard to obtain and harder to keep since there were easier ways to make money than as a craftsman. There were laws against manufacturing in the colonies that were occasionally enforced during the eighteenth century, but circumstances more than the law prevented success for ambitious efforts at manufacturing fine ceramics, glassware, or metal.

Right after the Revolution, when the new nation was forming, there seems to have been surprisingly little attention paid to becoming self-sufficient as far as producing luxuries was concerned. One or two attempts at glassmaking were undertaken, but there was relatively little effort to expand ceramics production. The re-establishment of relations with England brought easy access to inexpensive fine ceramics which were very quickly designed to appeal to the American market. Subtle preferences for color and ornamentation were understood by the English suppliers, and more obviously, decorative pieces with political motifs included a quantity of wares that had American patriotic pictures which were, on occasion, anti-British. The Staffordshire manufacturers wanted business and seemed willing to supply any demand. Certainly the creamware body lent itself best to transfer-print decoration, which included anti-British cartoons, and there was no better way to show the faults of the anti-British belief than by providing fine English products for the American market. It was difficult to compete with the British potteries that had mastered their art.

Nineteenth-Century Range

Documents provide evidence of the development of potteries producing finer earthenwares in the early nineteenth century, but unfortunately, up to this time there are no examples that have been securely identified. Perhaps the study of ceramics that have come down in families that would have had access to these potteries will help uncover new material. Because no marked pieces of American manufacture have been found to assist in identifying the wares, so far none are securely distinguished from the imports. There is a possibility that more will be learned about sophisticated American wares of the period. If so, problems of attribution for simpler wares will probably be clarified.

Creamware

In the early 1800s Philadelphia had a number of potteries that produced varied wares. As a large city (it had been one of the largest in the British Empire before the Revolution), it attracted many craftsmen. Its potters made wares of any type, and although the newspapers mention high-fired wares, it hasn't been possible to identify them unless marked. In 1808 examples of queen's ware (known also as creamware and the high-fired earthenware that Wedgwood had perfected in about 1760) made at the Columbian Pottery were exhibited at the Peale Museum. In the 1809 report to the legislature, the governor of Pennsylvania boasted that, "We have lately established in Philadelphia a queensware pottery on an extensive scale." The extent of efforts in this direction is difficult to ascertain. Several other potteries operating in Philadelphia at the time may have produced similar wares. The only positive evidence, however, refers to forms that may have been made of the lower-quality earthenwares. Black coffeepots, for example, which are mentioned in advertisements, were a red earthenware that was molded, inexpensive, and popular until the middle of the century.

In 1817, David G. Seixas, whose father had been the rabbi of the New York synagogue during the Revolution, was reported making Liverpool whitewares, a type of creamware. One piece attributed to him through family history is actually covered with a green glaze but is an example of higher-fired earthenware. Seixas' efforts in ceramics were only a minor part of his varied interests. For a while he headed a school for deaf-mutes, and he was involved in a scandal that many thought proved he was a victim of anti-Semitism.

Several famous names in ceramics of the Philadelphia area first came up in the beginning of the century, but no proof of what they were making is evident before the 1820s. In the first exhibition of The Franklin Institute in 1824, Abraham Miller, whose father had been potting in Philadelphia before 1790, displayed luster pitchers and specimens of porcelain and whiteware that showed the improvement of potteries in America. The judges' report was blissfully unmindful of shipping statistics when it stated, ". . . since our potters have attained the art of making it equal, if not superior, to the imported, and as cheap, they have entirely excluded the foreign ware from the American market."

One of the better-known names in Philadelphia ceramics is that of Thomas Haig. Haig had migrated from England in 1812 and made red and black wares as well as stonewares, although he had been trained to produce creamwares. The Second Annual Exhibition of The Franklin Institute in 1825 included specimens of both earthenware and stone-

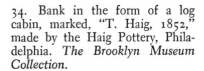

34. Bank in the form of a log cabin, marked, "T. Haig, 1852," made by the Haig Pottery, Philadelphia. *The Brooklyn Museum Collection.*

ware in coffeepots, pitchers, strainers, cake molds, and pans, "From clay taken in the city." The wares were admired by the judges who felt that their glazes were good and their bodies "perfectly burned and deprived of all absorbent qualities." The coffeepots were handsome Empire forms in black that have survived in some number. Haig made Rockingham wares, and one popular pitcher was decorated with a representation of Washington as a Mason. The Haig Pottery continued to operate all through the nineteenth century, although the founder died in 1833.

Yellowware

The first quarter of the nineteenth century was a period of extensive experimentation in the field of manufacturing. All over the young nation new ways were being adopted for making metal, cloth, glass, and ceramics. Since traditions were not strong, new ideas were quickly taken up. For ceramics, at first the basic concept of mass production inspired larger potteries with kilns that could be fired at higher temperatures, but few profound changes in method. Clays were purified better, fired when necessary at a higher temperature, but potters both turned and molded pieces as they had in smaller shops. Instead of progressing from red to yellowware, however, there was a broad increase in the number of wares made, and if Philadelphia is to be regarded as indicative of the activity in the smaller cities, earthenwares were made in great number, although the higher-fired wares were becoming increasingly important. For collectors, the period offers a great challenge because so few pieces of ceramics have been identified although the period is rich in documents.

Rockingham

The most typical nineteenth-century earthenware is Rockingham. It fits the preconception of a typical

nineteenth-century ware by being a proper combination of a rough-looking ware and sophisticated
relief ornament based on earlier styles. Developed
in late eighteenth-century England as a popular
rural ware, it is brown glazed on a high-fired earthenware body. The name is taken from the marquis
of Rockingham at whose pottery it is thought to
have originated. Essentially the glaze is a nineteenth-century version of the brown tortoise-shell
glaze used on so-called Whieldon wares (one of
the all-popular eighteenth-century Staffordshire substitutes for porcelain). The nineteenth-century
color is more intense than the earlier, but Rockingham glazes vary from plain, smooth dark brown to
the sponged effect of tortoise-shell by the addition
of green, blue, or yellow color. The characteristic
Rockingham pieces were most often molded, and
the molds were occasionally in complex sculptural
relief designs. Being a functional ware, ordinary
relatively plain dishes and bowls were made for
use as ovenware. Before gas and electric stoves,
cooking heat was not as high as it is today, so
it wouldn't be advisable to follow an old recipe in a
Rockingham piece.

One of the first potteries to produce Rockingham
in the United States was opened by D. & J. Henderson in about 1830. The Henderson brothers had
purchased the works of the Jersey Porcelain and
Earthenware Company in 1828 and exhibited at
The Franklin Institute annual show in 1830. The
"flint stoneware" on view then was of the thin
variety used for molded wares not unlike Rockingham. The stonewares were brown and buff objects,
molded with relief ornament. This was not very
different from the stoneware made in eighteenth-century Virginia, although the Hendersons probably
were following then current English vogues. Along
with various earthenware bodies, stoneware was used

35. Stoneware Toby jug by D. & J. Henderson, Jersey City, New Jersey, about 1830. *The Brooklyn Museum Collection.*

for thin-bodied decorative pieces close to Rockingham. One piece marked D. &. J. Henderson was their version of the Toby jug. This popularly sentimental and satirical representation of a pudgy sailor was of a type of humorous decorative ceramics that had been introduced in England in the 1760s. Other pitchers—squat forms with applied relief figures—were close to late eighteenth-century Staffordshire products, which had become accepted as traditional works.

The Staffordshire potteries, first employing the talents of a sculptor named Ralph Wood, began making small figures of a "homey, rural" type in the 1760s. The English figures were distinctive in their primitive quality, although not as naively executed as the examples that followed in the 1820s. The appeal was broad, and the Hendersons produced designs to appeal to the same taste. This thin stoneware body was also used for molded pitchers with hunting scenes that were in the fashion of 1830 in England and better known in the Rockingham glaze. The molds of these pitchers with hunting scenes are attributed to Daniel Greatbach, an English modeler who had migrated. He started his American career in Jersey City, and worked at the most important potteries in the decades that followed. The pitcher with a greyhound dog as handle and the scene of the battle between the deer and the dogs, first made by the

36. Rockingham-glazed molded earthenware teapot by Daniel Greatbach, American Pottery Company, Jersey City, New Jersey, 1840. *Collection of the Newark Museum.*

37. Rockingham-glazed earthenware Toby jug, American Pottery Company, Jersey City, New Jersey, 1840. *The Brooklyn Museum Collection.*

Hendersons, was repeated at many different factories in the latter part of the century.

In 1833 a reorganization of the Jersey City pottery by the Hendersons involved recapitalization and incorporation. The newly formed business was called American Pottery Manufacturing Company at first, and later, the American Pottery Company. The wares they made covered the broad range of useful and decorative work that was more rural than urban, if the country or rural scene is regarded as rustic and unfashionable. Actually, since the wares were less expensive than porcelain, it seemed possible to experiment and reflect more of the decorative ideas of the period than in porcelain. American porcelain, it will be seen later, was conservatively designed, while earthenware was more adventuresome.

The fashion in 1833 would be hard to define precisely. Designers tended to follow a variety of trends and to revive any one of a group of styles. Styles were more accurately defined as decorative motifs in the early nineteenth century, since they were a system of ornamentation rather than the basic method of design implied in earlier periods. The conservative trend favored the Empire style,

38. Stoneware pitcher with Rockingham glaze, American Pottery Company, Jersey City, New Jersey, about 1840. *Collection of the Newark Museum.*

and bold classical shapes in this spirit were employed. One coffeepot made in stoneware had applied decoration consisting of classical masks in acanthus-leaf borders around the main body with grapevine bands in the upper areas. The Gothic revival appealed to architects, cabinetmakers, and other craftsmen, and the English potters devised a popular "Apostles' Pitcher." At the American Pottery Company the apostles motif decorated a spittoon. Although it may be tempting for those who like to explain art politically to say that this was a device to inspire spitting on the apostles and an expression of the strong anti-Catholic movement in the United States about 1840, other theorists find it more reasonable to see it simply as an expression of interest in Gothic design. For some the Gothic inspiration was based on their feeling of the religious power of the style; for more it was a fascinating relief from the heavy classicism of the Empire style. Writers on design of the 1830s and '40s demanded consistency. If a room was to be "Grecian" (Empire), every detail was in the "Grecian" or Empire spirit, and if it was to be Gothic, then the same rule would hold. The spittoon was designed to match furniture and architectural

39. Stoneware cuspidor, American Pottery Company, Jersey City, New Jersey, about 1840. *The Brooklyn Museum Collection.*

trim. This is an unusual piece, but it helps to understand the design attitudes popular before the middle of the century.

The Gothic was not exclusive to the American Pottery Company, but was used by others into the 1850s. The pointed arch was a common motif on plain pitchers and spittoons; the apostles reappear at their grandest on a water cooler—made at Bennington for exhibition at the Crystal Palace in 1853 in New York—but then the Gothic went out of style along with the "Grecian," with which it had the closest affinity.

40. Rockingham earthenware pitcher, American Pottery Company, Jersey City, New Jersey, about 1840. *The Brooklyn Museum Collection.*

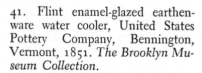

41. Flint enamel-glazed earthenware water cooler, United States Pottery Company, Bennington, Vermont, 1851. *The Brooklyn Museum Collection.*

The rococo revival was a third important style of the period in which the American Pottery Company flourished. A tea set they made epitomizes the characteristic approach. The set is known in an off-white-glazed stoneware, a yellow-glazed ware, and the brown-glazed Rockingham. The pieces are squat with naturalistic details, and the shapes reminiscent of oriental models. The small rose-vine pattern which serves as relief decoration, familiar in eighteenth-century rococo design, is also characteristic, but the nineteenth-century designer treated it more realistically than did his predecessor. Again, the motif is more of a decorative scheme than an artistic style. Historical precedent was the source of the ornament, but the conception and the forms were peculiar to the time in which it was made. The tea set was unusually fine for its time, for it was on a level of quality in both design and execution that was rarely achieved by contemporary potters.

The range of the efforts of the American Pottery Company was unusually extensive. Whiteware—high-fired earthenware with white-glazed surfaces—was attempted. This was the most popular dinnerware of the period. The imported whiteware with over-all blue transfer-print decoration was common. Quantities were made in Staffordshire for export to markets in both the Old and New Worlds. The transfer decoration consisted of a floral or leaf border with a scene in the center. English factories vied with each other for finding appealing scenes. American subjects were often used. Artists actually visited the United States in search of material at times, although prints were a more frequent source of inspiration. For collectors the American views are of great interest. It is peculiar that the one American effort to supply the demand for the popular blue-decorated whiteware has a romantic imaginary scene

42. Earthenware plate, Canova pattern, American Pottery Company, about 1840. *The Brooklyn Museum Collection.*

as its center subject. Made by the American Pottery Company it was marked as the Canova pattern. The scene, a free rendering of the theme, is bolder and plainer than the English models.

Another popular Staffordshire product with the same white-glazed body had sponged blue borders and transfer-print decoration for the center motif. American Pottery imitated this as well, showing that it was capable of making whatever Staffordshire did. Again the details were bolder, there was a crudeness that made it stand out, and for enthusiasts the American product is more distinctive and charming than the English.

The Jersey City pottery which had been taken over by D. & J. Henderson in 1828 was operated until David Henderson's death in 1845 as the American Pottery Manufacturing Company (1833–40) and as the American Pottery Company (1840–45). It set the standards and showed the range for earthenware in the period and, for the next few decades, served as a model followed by many potters. The factory continued to be operated from

1845 to 1854 by Rhodes, Strong and McGeron, who did not mark their wares. In 1859 Rouse and Turner produced white and cream-colored earthenwares along with Parian—a ware to be discussed later. They continued until 1892, marking their work with an imitation English mark that featured the British coat of arms and their initials.

A contemporary of the Hendersons, John Hancock, migrated from England to open a pottery in South Amboy, New Jersey, in 1828. Little more is known about what he produced other than that it was the yellow- and Rockingham-glazed wares. His credentials were impressive, for he had been an apprentice at Etruria (the Wedgwood factory) and a manager of the Clews factory. In 1840 he moved to Louisville, Kentucky, to make stoneware and the next year went on to East Liverpool, Ohio, where he made yellow- and Rockingham wares for a short time before his death in 1842. Hancock's story is similar to a number of others in the mid-nineteenth century which show that the industry received steady stimulation from English-trained potters who quickly moved west.

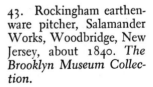

43. Rockingham earthenware pitcher, Salamander Works, Woodbridge, New Jersey, about 1840. *The Brooklyn Museum Collection.*

At Louisville, Kentucky, in 1829 the Lewis Pottery Company was founded to produce an ambitious group of wares, including both queen's ware and porcelain, and unquestionably did make both the yellow- and Rockingham wares. The enterprise was supplemented by the efforts of a pair of potters who had operated in Pittsburgh earlier. There are few surviving examples to show what was made, but it was doubtless in the spirit of the Jersey City efforts and a combination of popular rustic designs, with rococo-revival and Empire-style forms used. A variation in theme was the introduction of designs that were simple and primitive interpretations that may be regarded as folk art. One pottery whose mark is on the folklike examples is the Salamander pottery, which operated in Woodbridge, New Jersey, from 1825 to 1896. Its Rockingham was produced between 1836 and 1842 when Michel Lefoulon and Henry Decasse were in charge. They produced the typical hound-handled pitchers with hunting scenes in relief that are hard to attribute unless marked, as well as a ship scene that is plainly delineated and simplified like the Hudson River-scene paintings of the time. Not marked but very close in spirit and border is a pitcher whose squat form is decorated with a picturesque fire engine and firemen approaching a burning house. Again, the details are rendered with the simplicity of a folk artist.

The folk artist was the rare phenomenon in American Rockingham. As a sculptor with a definite notion of how to abbreviate form and still be meaningful he was successful, but his primitive touch was less ambitious than most potters cared to be. They could achieve more fashionable results by the easy expedient of making a mold from a piece manufactured by a rival. It required little

44. Rockingham-glazed earthenware pitcher, Taylor and Speeler, Trenton, New Jersey, 1852–56. *Collection of the Newark Museum.*

45. Rockingham earthenware pitcher, American Pottery Company, Jersey City, New Jersey, about 1840. *The Brooklyn Museum Collection.*

effort, and the results seemed sophisticated. The more ordinary molded wares are confusing because it is difficult to decide whether the quality of a mold is bad because it was too worn or simply a recent copy. The seemingly fashionable designs were in the spirit of academic painting and reflected similar sources. Seventeenth-century genre subjects, naturalistic floral and plant arrangements as well as the all-popular hunting scenes, are in a sense poor-man's romanticism and relate to more famous European painters like Delacroix and Géricault and the lesser known artists who painted "period" scenes. The work was done at potteries all over the country between about 1830 and 1860.

In New Jersey several other potteries at South Amboy are worthy of mention. One is the Swan Hill Pottery, probably established in 1849 and operated for a short time by Hanks & Fish (1850–51)

46. Rockingham earthenware pitcher by Abraham Cadmus, South Amboy, New Jersey, about 1850. *The Brooklyn Museum Collection.*

47. Rockingham-glazed earthenware batter jug by Abraham Cadmus, South Amboy, New Jersey, about 1850. *Collection of the Newark Museum.*

and then by James Carr (1852–54). The pottery made the usual hunting-scene pitchers but also cylindrically shaped ale pitchers that bore decorative bands of grapes and vines in relief. The Swan Hill Pottery was revived in about 1856 and operated after 1860 by J. L. Rue and Company, who repeated some of the early designs.

Another South Amboy pottery, the Congress Pottery, operated by Abraham Cadmus between 1849 and 1854, produced Rockingham glazed wares in rococo-revival, Gothic, and rustic designs. One figure, a bull reclining, is attributed to Daniel Greatbach, who is regarded as the ablest ceramic modeler of American scenes.

In tracing the history of the individuals responsible for the growth of the American ceramics industry, mobility is frequently found to be a factor. Potters migrated from England, settled for a time in New Jersey, and then sought greater fortune away from the established centers by going to New

48. Rockingham-glazed earthenware bull calf by Abraham Cadmus, South Amboy, New Jersey, about 1850. *The Brooklyn Museum Collection.*

England, the Midwest, or the South. There were a surprising number of attempts to start potteries, with successful businessmen in a locality financing a potter from Clews, Etruria, or some other familiar English manufacturer whose name marked the bottoms of plates on American tables. For the aspiring capitalist it seemed too easy—a pat of mud, skilled hands, and a fire might lead to a fortune. The mud, which was potentially everywhere, rarely was right for manufacturing yellowware; hands often lacked all the skills needed; fire took a lot more fuel than anyone would have guessed. For aspiring collectors it might be interesting to read local histories of their home towns—the commemorative volumes that would have been written to celebrate a milestone: a centennial, the golden anniversary, or the opening of a railroad station. It is one way to find out if a pottery was attempted. If so, one could try to find its output.

Success for potters required good raw materials, a fuel supply, skilled management, and good transportation. One of the centers developed in the Midwest having all the proper qualities was East Liverpool, Ohio, which was mentioned earlier in a description of John Hancock's peregrinations.

East Liverpool, Ohio, had its first important pottery in 1839 when James Bennett opened it. He produced yellowware and, growing quickly, was joined by several brothers in 1841. The going must have been tough, because the able Bennetts did not last long, although East Liverpool became the "Trenton of the West" before the end of the century. By 1844 the brothers had decided to relocate in order to expand and went to Birmingham, Pennsylvania (now a part of Pittsburgh). Their submissions to the exhibitions of both The Franklin Institute of Philadelphia and the American Institute of New York were rewarded with prizes.

49. Earthenware teapot, "Rebekah at the Well," E. & W. Bennett, Baltimore, Maryland, about 1850. *The Brooklyn Museum Collection.*

One of the brothers, Edwin, established a pottery in Baltimore in 1846, where for a while he was joined by another brother, William. They made a teapot with a representation of "Rebekah at the Well" between 1851 and at least until 1900 that was unusually popular. At the 1853 Crystal Palace they exhibited a patented blue majolica pitcher which had the sea life of the Chesapeake Bay as its subject in relief decoration. This was not very appealing if sales records be used as an indicator.

The pottery the Bennetts left behind in East Liverpool was operated by the Croxalls afterward, and John W. Croxall and Sons made Rockingham until at least 1900. A number of manufacturers thrived in the town from about 1840 or '50 on, and some are continuing. Gradually after the 1870s they shifted from Rockingham to granite or ironstone. Harker, Taylor, Goodwin, Baggott, McNicol, Rigby, Salt, Mear, Woodward, Blakely, Brunt, Marley, Knowles, and Vodrey are among the significant names in East Liverpool. Production centered on functional wares but included some fine porcelain.

The synonym for Rockingham among American collectors is Bennington, the scene of significant activity in the middle of the nineteenth century. The individual who did the most to create the reputation for this Vermont town was Christopher Webber Fenton, who was responsible for much experimentation and the more adventuresome products attempted at Bennington.

Bennington, Vermont, was just another town where potteries would not have been successful before transportation improved. Local clays were not too good, although stoneware began to be a profitable industry quite early in the century. Christopher Webber Fenton was the son of a potter, Jonathan, who had been in business in Dorset, Vermont. Having married into a Bennington family of potters, the Nortons, the younger Fenton moved there in about 1835. He patented a firebrick in 1837, which was sold by the Nortons at their Bennington Stone Ware Factory, so that he probably was associated with the factory before he formed

50. Flint enamel-glazed earthenware sugar bowl, Lyman, Fenton & Company, Bennington, Vermont, about 1850. *The Brooklyn Museum Collection.*

51. Flint enamel-glazed earthenware dog, Lyman, Fenton & Company, Bennington, Vermont, about 1850. *The Metropolitan Museum of Art, The Rogers Fund, 1913.*

a partnership with Julius Norton in 1842 or 1843. Norton and Fenton were in business until 1847, and among their marked wares are examples of the earliest New England Rockingham. The marked pieces are hexagonal-shaped pitchers with floral ornament in relief.

Evidently one reason for dissolving the partnership was a difference of opinion on how far they should go in making decorative pieces. At any rate, the year after Norton and Fenton had terminated their agreement, Fenton had become a member of Lyman, Fenton & Park. Their main interest was dry goods, but they also described themselves in a newspaper advertisement as "manufacturers of every description of Rockingham, White Flint and White Earthen, Crockery Ware—East Bennington, Vt."

By the end of 1849, Park was no longer connected and Fenton had obtained another patent. This new patent was for coloring the glaze by sprinkling metallic oxides on wares. Tones of blue, yellow, and orange were blended with the mottled browns of ordinary Rockingham in a fine durable surface. The familiar oval mark, Lyman, Fenton & Co./Fenton's/Enamel/Patented/1849/Bennington, Vt., was used for all Rockingham wares, not only during the partnership, which lasted until 1852, but for some time later.

The patented ware impressed one writer, who, in reporting on porcelain and ceramic manufacture at the Crystal Palace Exhibition of 1853, said that it was made of very white South Carolina clay. Fenton's version of Rockingham is a particularly fine ware that was made along with a variety of more ambitious products.

Fenton's last enterprise at Bennington was the United States Pottery Company, which was incorporated in 1853. Lyman had been associated with Fenton until 1852, and a new large pottery had been erected by the partners. The new corporation had brought new capital into the enterprise at a period when porcelains were made. The Rockingham glazes produced continued earlier forms, as well as going into a few remarkable figures. By 1849, the range of wares, besides pitchers, bowls, and a line of functional dishes, included candlesticks, frames, doorknobs, soap dishes, water coolers, tea sets, and related objects in the typical glazes. Later came the introduction of more elaborate molds, traditionally associated with the work of Daniel Greatbach, the modeler who had worked in New Jersey and was in Bennington from 1852. Whether he could have done all that is attributed to him is open to question. The United States Pottery Company made some elaborate sculptural forms. The range of flasks included examples shaped like books and others in the form of coachmen. The United States Pottery version of the traditional pitchers with hunting scenes and greyhound handles

52. Flint enamel-glazed earthenware lion, United States Pottery Company, Bennington, Vermont, about 1855. *The Brooklyn Museum Collection.*

was particularly vital. The dogs are rendered in tense positions, with their heads up and bodies articulated to accentuate muscles and potential movement. R. C. Barret, director of the Bennington Museum, has contrasted true and false Bennington by pointing out how other potteries made the greyhound handles flat and almost abstract, with no suggestion of movement. Many of the contemporary variations are more stylized and less successful. Toby jugs, which also had been familiar products, were more vital in Bennington examples.

The list of animals is headed by lions, which occasionally bear the 1849 mark. These were evidently not often imitated in American potteries. Deer, the stag and doe paired off, were another popular type bearing the 1849 mark. Poodles carrying baskets and cows reclining like the deer or standing to serve as creamers were also popular figures made in Bennington. Although best known in Rockingham ware, the figures were sometimes repeated in finer bodies.

The broad range of Bennington forms and the variety of decorative motifs makes it epitomize design in its period. Empire-style designs, along with

53. Flint enamel-glazed earthenware doe, United States Pottery Company, Bennington, Vermont, about 1855. *The Metropolitan Museum of Art, The Rogers Fund, 1938.*

54. Flint enamel-glazed earthenware stag, United States Pottery Company, Bennington, Vermont, about 1855. *The Metropolitan Museum of Art, The Rogers Fund, 1938.*

the rococo revival, remained important until the closing of the United States Pottery, but perhaps most significant for the Rockingham wares were the primitive rustic designs in the tradition that had begun in the Staffordshire region in the 1760s and continued in the nineteenth century.

Rockingham continued to enjoy a popularity through the 1860s and 1870s, with earlier designs retaining their popularity. As technology improved and white and colored glazes were introduced, the need for Rockingham subsided, replaced by imitations of porcelain. The brightly colored majolica that had been introduced in the 1850s was more popular in the 1880s. E. & W. Bennett of Baltimore introduced a patented majolica body with a pitcher they exhibited at the New York Crystal Palace Exhibition of 1853. The glaze is light blue, and its relief surface features representations of the underwater life from Chesapeake Bay. Made at a variety of potteries, but typified by the firm of Griffin,

55. Majolica earthenware pitcher, E. & W. Bennett, Baltimore, Maryland, 1853. *The Brooklyn Museum Collection.*

Hill and Smith, Phoenixville, Pennsylvania, majolica was inspired particularly by eighteenth-century models. The well-known cauliflower-shaped majolica teapot repeats a design Wedgwood used at the beginning of his career. Floral bowls and compotes are freer variations of earlier models made to appeal in the 1880s by employing a pale, pretty palette.

Graniteware and Ironstone

At first glance, the white-glazed, decorated graniteware and ironstone are hard to distinguish from the English wares of the time. Hard wares developed from creamware, they are gray-white that is ornamented with over-all patterns, often handsomely colored. Dinner sets and bedroom sets to go on washstands reflect fashions of the time. At their most attractive, the designs have the lightness of contemporary textiles, and motifs are generally the mixture of floral and architectural patterns that might be named neo-rococo to distinguish them from the earlier, heavier and more realistic rococo revival.

Eclecticism, the major style of the 1880s, influenced forms and designs. Near Eastern shapes and motifs were combined with the classical in new conceptions.

The field has been largely neglected, so that it takes careful searching to come up with examples marked by American potteries. It is an area of collecting that should be fascinating as a pioneering venture because there is a lot of very corny material to be separated from fine designs.

The late nineteenth and twentieth centuries marked the success of American ceramics from the technological point of view. Factories were able to make any product that was desired, and although the design of the period has yet to be studied in sufficient detail, forms followed the fashions with

56. Earthenware pitcher, Millington, Astbury and Poulson, Trenton, New Jersey, 1861. *The Brooklyn Museum Collection.*

some distinction. Again, with a proper understanding of the trends of the time, the adventuresome collector may find significant American examples. The historical revivals of the early twentieth century are a phenomenon that must be studied. Art nouveau, the experimental style of the period, was less important, since it appealed to a relatively small group.

Later the modern style, which was popularized at the Paris Exposition in 1927, was as much reflected in the inexpensive ceramics as in the expensive musical films of the 1930s. As objects get closer in time, it becomes more difficult to be sufficiently detached to judge them without emotional reactions based on experiences which have nothing to do with aesthetics.

CHAPTER V

Porcelain

Porcelain has always had a special exotic aura. The word itself is from the Italian word, *porcellana,* meaning cowrie shell. Traditionally the term was thought to have been used for the first time in reference to a ceramic body by Marco Polo when he exclaimed in wonder at first seeing the material during his travels in the Orient. Porcelain is made of two special ingredients, kaolin and feldspar, which can be fired more highly than other types of clay. The high temperature of the kiln bakes the materials to an extremely hard consistency, so that porcelain is at once more durable and more delicate than other ceramics.

Porcelain was made first in China about the ninth century A.D., and isolated Chinese examples reached the West by the twelfth century. Trade with the West increased during the Ming Dynasty (1368–1644), and Chinese porcelain became better known to Europeans.

The first attempt to make porcelain in the West took place in the fifteenth century. One major problem was analyzing the ingredients. Glass was mistakenly thought to be the material for the glass-like surface. Glass and clay combinations—called soft-paste porcelain—required less heat than kaolin and feldspar, but the results were less durable. The first European porcelain was made in Florence in blue and white designs modeled after then current oriental fashions. Seventeenth-century efforts were similar, although at French factories in Rouen and St. Cloud, soft-paste porcelain was produced in designs inspired by both oriental models and fashionable metalwork.

The discovery of the secret of true porcelain was made by Johann Friedrich Böttger, an alchemist who was working for the Elector of Saxony at Meissen, near Dresden. The first porcelain was made there in 1713. Böttger had had a colorful career earlier, claiming he could produce gold from base materials, and making porcelain was a means of saving his neck. In spite of all precautions for secrecy the Meissen technique was learned elsewhere. In the course of the first half of the eighteenth century other factories began producing porcelain.

First Attempts in America

Two Western accounts of Chinese factories making porcelain were published in the first half of the eighteenth century. One by Father d'Entrecolles and the other by du Halde were influential in assisting aspiring occidental porcelain makers. According to some sources, one reader of du Halde's *Description of the Empire of China*, Andrew Duché, began to develop American porcelain. Knowing the ingredients and techniques of making porcelain from his reading, Duché, a Savannah potter, made experiments that led to his discovery of local supplies of the right materials for making porcelain. The French edition had come out in 1735, and there would have been time to search before the governor of Georgia reported on December 29, 1739, that:

> Andrew Duché is the Potter at Savannah who . . . had made several Experiments which seem to look like the making of China.

A later report by the secretary of the Colony described Duché's work as translucent. The few pieces attributed to Duché which have turned up are blue and white porcelain. The venture was not a success. Duché was last mentioned attempting to sell American clays in England.

Other attempts to produce porcelain are mentioned closer to the eve of the Revolution, in the 1760s and 1770s. The Germantown (later known as Quincy), Massachusetts, pottery, operated in the 1760s by Richard Cranch and Joseph C. Palmer, produced thin-bodied wares that might have been porcelain. The fragments that Edwin Atlee Barber reported seeing in the 1890s would have to be located to be re-examined. The very existence of it has been challenged by Lura Woodside Watkins, who was of the opinion that fragments found at Germantown were very likely household breakage. Mrs. Watkins reported she found no evidence of potters in the Germantown community, although earlier writers mentioned them.

In the case of Samuel Bowen, who was awarded a prize by the American Society for the Encouragement of Arts and Manufactures "for his useful observations in china," some question has also been raised. Was it his discovery of the good clay that won him an award, or was he really responsible for making porcelain? No examples of his work have come down, but Alice Morse Earle quoted from Felix Farley's *Bristol Journal*, November 24, 1764:

"This week, some pieces of porcelain manufactured in Georgia was imported; the materials appear to be good, but the workmanship is far from being admired." Another attempt recorded in the South was that of John Bartlam, an English potter who settled in South Carolina. Bartlam announced his intentions of opening a "China Manufactory and Pottery" in October, 1770. By the end of January he was making queen's ware and saying he "Will be much obliged to Gentlemen in the Country, or others, who will be so kind to send him samples of any kinds of fine Clay upon their Plantations . . ." No further word was heard from Bartlam, so that he probably never did make porcelain. Josiah Wedgwood, who was concerned that American manufacturing might hurt his business, seemed relieved to find that his competition in South Carolina was ". . . one of our insolvent master potters," who, we may assume, was John Bartlam.

The most fruitful effort in eighteenth-century American porcelain manufacture occurred in Philadelphia, where on December 29, 1769, and January 1, 1770, newspapers announced:

New China Ware. Notwithstanding the various difficulties and disadvantages which usually attend the introduction of any important manufacture into a new country, the proprietors of the China-works now erecting in Southwark have the pleasure to acquaint the public that they have proved to a certainty that the clays of America are as productive of good porcelain as any heretofore manufactured at the famous factory in Bow near London . . .

Unfortunately neither their clientele nor later students of ceramics were convinced of the quality of their product. The proprietors, Gousse Bonnin, probably from Antigua, and George Morris of Phil-

57. Porcelain (?) sweetmeat dish, Bonnin and Morris, Philadelphia, 1771. *The Brooklyn Museum Collection.*

adelphia, operated until 1772, although Morris withdrew in 1771. Bonnin left the country when the factory closed. The problems which beset the firm are suggested by their appeal for assistance in January, 1771, which was addressed to the Pennsylvania Assembly. Probably out of desperation they planned a lottery that was to be held in New Castle, Delaware, in December of that year.

The examples of work from the Bonnin and Morris factory that have survived are fairly thick, so that the composition of the body has been questioned. Through analysis of particles from a piece, bone ash has been found to be a significant component, and this suggests that a bone or softpaste porcelain was made. The advertisements mentioned "enamelled ware," which meant that polychrome decoration was used along with the more familiar blue decoration on the whiteware.

The wares that have been attributed to Bonnin and Morris reflect the influence of the Bow factory, which was mentioned in the first advertisement. The major difference is in the thickness of the ceramic body and the general grossness of the American pieces. Considering how much grosser the products of Bow and other English houses are in comparison

with the finer continental factories, American porcelain has understandably been confused with earthenware. On the other hand, the differences between
American and English porcelain are closely related
to the differences between American and English
work in other media. American porcelain design in
about 1770 was in the rococo style, but like American rococo design in furniture and silver, it was
heavier than its counterparts by English craftsmen.
The American spirit seems to have been best expressed in forthright designs that are bold and
gross. The sweetmeat dish of shells by Bonnin and
Morris (at the Brooklyn Museum) is very close
to one made at Bow but is heavier in each detail.

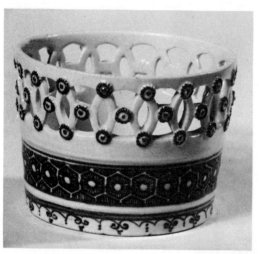

58. Porcelain (?) bon-
bon dish, Bonnin and
Morris, Philadelphia,
1771. *The Yale University
Art Gallery, Mabel Brady
Garvan Collection.*

59. Porcelain (?) sauceboat, Bonnin and Morris, Philadelphia, 1771.
The Brooklyn Museum Collection.

The Philadelphia Museum fruit bowl in the form of an open-weave basket, which was securely documented, is another example that is a heavier version of an English porcelain model. The sauceboat has relief scroll ornament framing blue oriental landscapes, which is an apt combination of the classical and oriental, characteristic of the rococo wherever it occurs. The Bonnin and Morris factory produced the only porcelain whose dates of manufacture are securely documented before the Revolution.

As the single effort that involved the fashion of the time, it reveals how consistent American designers were, regardless of what medium they used. In attributing more to contemporary factories it is important to test the approach. The English wares from the lesser factories that are sometimes crude and which might be confused with American products are invariably thinner and more intricately detailed than known work by Bonnin and Morris.

Nineteenth-Century Efforts

After the Revolution there was a radical change in style. The whimsical, asymmetrical rococo gave way to the more symmetrical, logical, and linear neoclassical style. The first phase of this style, which was delicate and linear, is not known in American porcelain. One company, the Boston Porcelain and Glass Company, was incorporated in 1814 with ambitious plans, but the porcelain department was reported to be a complete failure. Reference to a Philadelphia factory operating about 1800 is unsubstantiated, except in an account of a murder at the "China Factory" in 1800. This may have been the closed Bonnin and Morris factory as easily as an active plant.

Dr. Mead

The earliest evidence of porcelain manufacture after the Revolution was in 1816, when Dr. Henry

Mead operated a factory which was probably located in New York. By that time neoclassicism had changed. The pendulum of taste had swung from finding appeal in the delicate to a demand for heavier proportions. Symmetry and logic continued to prevail in designs, but results were closer to the ancient classical inspiration. Dr. Mead's single surviving piece was preserved in The Franklin Institute with a note that dated it 1816. Dr. Mead was a New York physician who petitioned the New York Common Council, December 11, 1820, to investigate the advantages of allowing him to employ paupers and criminals. This ingenious idea was more than likely predicated on the good doctor's inability to pay potters and painters, and it is not surprising that there is only one piece of this porcelain now known. The piece is an urn-shaped vase with caryatid handles in the spirit of Paris work of the time. In J. Leander Bishop's *History of American Manufactures*, the starting date of the Mead enterprise is given as 1819. In his obituary the factory was said to be in New Jersey, so there evidently is still a lot to be learned about Dr. Mead.

In 1824 at The Franklin Institute, Abraham Miller of Philadelphia exhibited a specimen of porcelain along with a variety of other wares. Miller's porcelain was considered fine, but most of his production was concentrated on larger-scale wares, such as portable furnaces and fire bricks. The Miller porcelain has not been preserved, but a dinner set by John Vickers, signed and dated 1824, still exists. The forms of the set are in part the plain forms characteristic of the Empire style, but rococo pieces are also included. The simple fruit still lifes that are painted on the plates are also in the Empire style and in the spirit of fruit painted or carved on furniture of the time. Vickers is recorded as a

60. Porcelain plate by John Vickers, Chester County, Pennsylvania, 1824. *The Brooklyn Museum Collection.*

61. Porcelain perfume vials by William Ellis Tucker, Philadelphia, 1826. *The Brooklyn Museum Collection.*

potter in Chester County, Pennsylvania, and although the set was found in England with no known connecting link to the American potter except his name, the porcelain body is convincingly close to later products of Chester County clay.

Another documented factory was the Jersey Porcelain and Earthenware Company. Organized in 1825, it won a silver medal in 1826 at The Franklin Institute. A bold simple piece with gold decoration was once identified as an example of Jersey Porcelain but is now lost.

Tucker
Porcelain

American porcelain in the Empire style was at its best in the output of the factory William Ellis Tucker opened in 1826. Tucker's father was a china merchant, and he had gained experience painting china before getting on with the more serious challenge of producing the ware. Tucker had several partners at different moments in the history of the enterprise. John Bird was in at the inception but was never active in the business. Thomas Hulme bought into the business in 1828, and although he was active for less than a year, there are pieces marked Tucker & Hulme. Alexander Hemphill came into the firm in 1831, and the new money enabled the pottery to enlarge. When William died in 1832, Alexander's father, Judge Joseph Hemphill, took over the company and retained Thomas Tucker (William's brother) as manager. In 1838 the pottery was closed.

Tucker porcelain is a handsome ware of some variety. Its forms are generally distinctively classical. Its decoration ranges from simple sepia to elaborate gilt and polychrome designs. Having won its first

62. Porcelain pitcher by William Ellis Tucker, Philadelphia, about 1830. *The Brooklyn Museum Collection.*

63. Porcelain plate, Tucker and Hemphill, Philadelphia, about 1835. *The Brooklyn Museum Collection.*

award at The Franklin Institute in 1827, Tucker porcelain was consistently fine in the twelve years it was produced. The judges' description is apt in saying: ". . . the body of this ware appeared to be strong, and sufficiently well fired, the glaze generally very good, the gilding executed in a neat and workmanlike manner." The factory produced tea sets, dinner sets, pitchers, vases, night light and teapot combinations, and a number of small vessels.

In the range of Tucker wares it is easiest to understand the style in examining typical pitchers. The basic form is an urn of Greco-Roman origin which has been modified into a pitcher. The ancient model would have been metal or a black ceramic

64. Pair of porcelain vases, Tucker and Hemphill, Philadelphia, about 1835. *The Valley Forge Historical Society.*

65. Porcelain pitcher, Tucker and Hemphill, Philadelphia, about 1835. *Private Collection.*

66. Porcelain jardiniere, Tucker and Hemphill, Philadelphia, about 1835. *The Metropolitan Museum of Art, The Rogers Fund, 1959.*

67. Porcelain pitcher, Smith, Fife & Co., Philadelphia, 1830. *The Brooklyn Museum Collection.*

68. A collection of porcelain from *The Henry Ford Museum, Dearborn, Michigan.* Left to right: 1. Pitcher, Tucker & Hulme, Philadelphia, Pa. 1828. 2. Pitcher, "Continental" Union Porcelain Works, Greenpoint, 1860. 3. Pitcher, water-lily pattern, United States Pottery Company, Bennington, Vermont, 1855. 4. Dish, Knowles, Taylor & Knowles, East Liverpool, Ohio, 1880.

urn. The nineteenth-century interpretation used a white ground with colored decoration. Some of the most handsome examples are decorated with floral garlands characteristic of the period. Local scenes and political heroes are other popular subjects featured in decoration on Tucker ware.

The 1830s were a time when another porcelain manufacturer, Smith, Fife & Co., was operating. Records show later activity in Philadelphia of which few examples survive. Ralph Bagnall Beach was awarded a patent for inlaying china in 1851, but a sample of the invention has not been preserved. Kurbaum and Schwartz made colorful wares at about the same time in Philadelphia.

The conservatism of American porcelain design may be explained by the fact that it was treasured too much for patrons to be satisfied with experimental design. Although the rococo revival had become popular in the design of molded wares, in porcelain the Empire style retained its importance until almost 1850.

Bennington

One of the first potteries to attempt to make rococo-revival porcelain was Norton and Fenton in Bennington, Vermont. They employed John Harrison, who is said to have worked for Copland when Parian was developed there. He worked on porcelain experiments but left before production was started. It would appear that the first production porcelain was made after the partnership of Norton and Fenton was dissolved and when the mark, Fenton's Works, would be applied, or in the 1847–58 period. (Actually the mark was occasionally used later, so questions can be raised about early dating.)

In the period between 1847 and 1858 the enterprises in which Christopher Webber Fenton was involved were responsible for producing a variety of porcelain, both glazed and biscuit. The biscuit or unglazed is often called Parian, after the ware perfected by Copland which had been developed as a sculptural medium and was supposedly reminiscent of Parian marble. Some hold that the American product is not fine enough to merit the name, but this seems a little too fussy. The Fenton enterprises also used colored clays in biscuit which are Victorian versions of Wedgwood jasper, with colors more intense than the pale hues dictated by eighteenth-century taste. Many of the imitations of Bennington biscuit had colors applied after firing.

Bennington porcelains are a broadly varied group. Functional porcelains for hotels and restaurants

69. Parian pitcher, "Cascade," United States Pottery Company, Bennington, Vermont, about 1855. *The Brooklyn Museum Collection.*

were made (but imitations of graniteware were also available) along with purely decorative figures and boxes and the like for use in bedrooms and parlors. Designs were devised to appeal to every taste. English competitors were copied with care, and new pieces were conceived. There was a quality in details that revealed the talents of those involved, but some of the routine repetitions of Staffordshire figures must have been as dull in 1850 as they are today. How to explain the mediocrity is more of a challenge than discussing the fine work. The dullest repetitions of badly conceived models are as authentic as the fine innovatory wares.

The best designs of the United States Pottery Company were conceived for the Parian body, which is at its most impressive when decoration is in high relief and details are rendered crisply. The cascade pitcher is a great example of the fine attention given details. It is in the naturalistic vein so popular in the rococo revival. The corn pitchers are examples in which a popular topical subject—one of the symbols of the nation—was used in a conservative classical form. Flowers and plants were occasionally chosen because they were exotic but always to fit the naturalistic tendency of the rococo. A sad moralistic tale, such as Paul and Virginia, in which a young pair perish for principles, appealed to the romantic taste of the times. The design was a further reflection of the rococo. Innocent praying children, Hiram Power's famous "Greek Slave," and a multitude of small ornamental pieces were handled with distinction, while indistinct, gross figures in the spirit of the worst Staffordshire figures were evidently made to supply a demand for bad design that has always seemed to have great commercial sales possibilities. The United States Pottery closed in 1858.

70. Parian pitchers, United States Pottery Company, Bennington, Vermont, 1850. *The Brooklyn Museum Collection.*

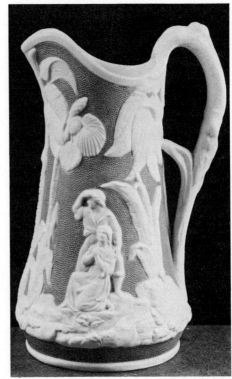

71. Biscuit-porcelain pitcher, "Paul and Virginia," United States Pottery Company, Bennington, Vermont, about 1855. *The Brooklyn Museum Collection.*

Greenpoint

In 1848 Charles Cartlidge opened a porcelain factory at Greenpoint, Brooklyn, which was operated until 1856. His output included buttons, umbrella and cane handles, and candlesticks, as well as the more usual dinner sets and pitchers. A particularly rare group of bisque busts and plaques were evidently done for the family. Most characteristic of Cartlidge are the pitchers he executed in a glossy glazed porcelain with acorn and oak leaves forming a popular decorative motif. The squat shape and the decoration are both reinterpreted rococo designs modified for nineteenth-century function and taste. The oak leaf may have appealed because of the fame of Connecticut's Charter Oak. Cartlidge

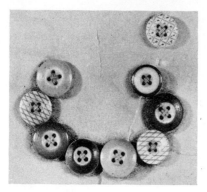

72. Porcelain buttons, Charles Cartlidge & Company, Greenpoint, New York, about 1850. *The Brooklyn Museum Collection.*

73. Porcelain candlestick, attributed to Charles Cartlidge & Company, Greenpoint, New York, about 1850. *The Brooklyn Museum Collection.*

74. Porcelain Toby cup with cover, Charles Cartlidge & Company, Greenpoint, New York, about 1850. *The Yale University Art Gallery, 1931.*

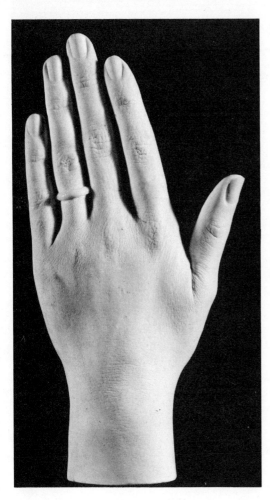

75. Hand of Ann Cart-
lidge Tyndale, by Charles
Cartlidge & Company,
Greenpoint, New York,
about 1850. *The Brooklyn
Museum Collection, lent
by a descendant.*

also did a corn pitcher, which was very different
from the Bennington example. Its clusters of corn
were more haphazard and seemingly rococo than
the Parian example. Cartlidge's sculptor, his brother-
in-law, Josiah Jones, was responsible for a limited
range of surviving designs.

The Cartlidge firm must have found competition
close when a second porcelain factory opened in
Greenpoint in 1853. William Boch and Brother
marked their wares with their name but also op-

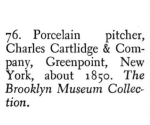

76. Porcelain pitcher, Charles Cartlidge & Company, Greenpoint, New York, about 1850. *The Brooklyn Museum Collection.*

erated as Empire or Union Porcelain. They and Cartlidge displayed their work at the Crystal Palace Exhibition in New York in 1853. The Boch company produced a variety of trimmings for doors, shutters, drawers, and stair rods, as well as the more expected pitchers. One pitcher is the perfect example of the rococo revival with a Bacchic figure sitting in a grape arbor in relief on glossy white porcelain.

Also in 1853 Morrison and Carr, operating as the New York City Pottery, opened a pottery in New York which included porcelain in its line. One partner, James Carr, had a particularly distinguished record in experimenting with improvements in design. Before the business was closed in 1888, they had made fine Parian busts as well as ornamental pieces that were at times lavishly decorated.

New Jersey   In the several other efforts that are recorded, American porcelain making seems to have been restricted to the rococo revival, showing little spirit of innovation. The American Porcelain Manufactur-

77. Porcelain pitcher, Charles Cartlidge & Company, Greenpoint, New York, about 1850. *The Brooklyn Museum Collection.*

78. Porcelain pitcher, Charles Cartlidge & Company, Greenpoint, New York, about 1850. *The Brooklyn Museum Collection.*

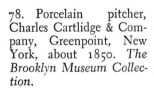

79. Porcelain pitcher, Charles Cartlidge & Company, Greenpoint, New York, about 1850. *The Brooklyn Museum Collection.*

80. Porcelain pitcher, William Boch and Brother, Greenpoint, New York, about 1853. *The Brooklyn Museum Collection.*

81. Porcelain pitcher, American Porcelain Manufacturing Company, Gloucester, New Jersey, about 1855. *The Brooklyn Museum Collection.*

ing Company, organized in 1854 at Gloucester, New Jersey (and operated after a few years as the Gloucester China Company), produced nice but hardly extraordinary pitchers with chinoiserie decoration before closing in 1860. The Southern Porcelain Manufacturing Company was organized in 1856 by a former partner in the United States Pottery Company of Bennington, Vermont, William H. Farrar, and employed Josiah Jones, who had been at Charles Cartlidge's Greenpoint pottery. Its output was not broad, but it included high-fired earthenwares. By the advent of the Civil War the concentration was on industrial parts for telegraphs and water pipes, but for a few years tablewares were made. The pieces identified include the corn pitcher that was also made at the Cartlidge plant.

The Civil War caused an interruption in the history of porcelain, as it did in many other aspects of American life. It occurred at a time when taste was changing and new ideas were becoming effective. The English theorist William Morris, for example, decried the low state of design in the decorative arts. He was against historicism—the approach to design which involved reviving earlier styles—and the misunderstanding of basic elements of design that were related to contemporary mass production. Morris had started a decorating company in London and attempted to inspire innovation in the decorative arts. Although he and his followers were known in the United States in the late 1860s, it was not until the Philadelphia Centennial Exhibition of 1876 that changes became apparent.

The new style is best described as eclectic. It was in the main made up of new combinations of traditional motifs. Oriental decorative themes were mixed with Western motifs to achieve new effects. Shapes derived from Middle Eastern brasses were used. The design patterns were often traditional but sometimes were based on mosaics and ceramics of the Middle East, too. Japanese porcelain, which had been imported in quantity, was also the inspiration for some of the more ambitious American efforts.

Technical experiments interested the manufacturers, who constantly improved the ceramic bodies they used. This interest in the chemical and mechanical elements of porcelain was not unique to Americans. At Sèvres the head of the company for several decades in the nineteenth century was a chemist, Brogniart. It seemed to be an expression of the bewilderment experienced by designers and manufacturers as well as their clients in the nineteenth century.

In about 1862, Thomas C. Smith took over the Union Porcelain Works. He had studied the techniques of porcelain making in Europe and was able to introduce hard-paste or true porcelain to replace the more usual soft-paste or bone porcelain. The output of the Union Porcelain Works in the 1860s

82. Porcelain vase, Union Porcelain Works, Greenpoint, New York, about 1880. *The Brooklyn Museum Collection, lent by Franklin Chace.*

was more or less a continuation of what had been made earlier, with gradual additions in tablewares. Underglaze colors were used for decoration as an innovation to improve upon the overglaze coloring familiar in work by Tucker and other earlier porcelain factories. Generally speaking, Union Porcelain was conservative, and its most significant decorative work followed earlier traditions.

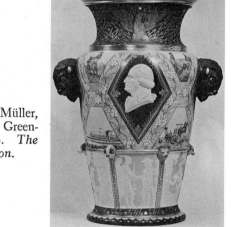

83. Porcelain vase by Karl Müller, Union Porcelain Works, Greenpoint, New York, 1876. *The Brooklyn Museum Collection.*

84. Part of a porcelain tea set, Union Porcelain Works, Greenpoint, New York, about 1875. *The Brooklyn Museum Collection, lent by Franklin Chace.*

85. Biscuit-porcelain bust of Pierre Van Arsdale Smith by Karl Müller, Union Porcelain Works, about 1880. *The Brooklyn Museum Collection, lent by Franklin Chace.*

The most interesting work of the Union Porcelain Works was done just before the Philadelphia Centennial. Karl Müller, a sculptor, supplied designs for an extensive group of wares to be exhibited in Philadelphia. First, the vase commemorating the Centennial epitomizes the conservatism of Union Porcelain. Taking the form of a classical urn, it was decorated in both color and relief. A profile of Washington in biscuit is dominant, and there are heads of the animals of North America used as punctuation around the piece on the bands that divide it into areas decorated with scenes. Biscuit is used for historic vignettes such as the Boston Tea Party, an Indian, and a Continental soldier. Contemporary scenes documenting progress by showing the building of the Brooklyn Bridge, factory scenes, and the like are painted. In a cup Müller designed, the handle represents Liberty, the

86. Biscuit-porcelain figure of blacksmith by Karl Müller, Union Porcelain Works, about 1880. *The Brooklyn Museum Collection, lent by Franklin Chace.*

87. Porcelain pitcher with portraits of poets, Union Porcelain Works, Greenpoint, New York, 1877. *The Brooklyn Museum Collection.*

Phrygian-capped female figure that Delacroix used, and biscuit reliefs of Mercury and Justice are around the sides of the piece, which has a high foot and a flaring lip, a shape suggesting a Near Eastern source. A tea set is conservative in its handsome floral decoration but tasteless in the choice of finials, which are a Negro head for the sugar and a Chinese head, complete with pigtail, for the teapot. The attempt to keep up with the trends is evident in a vase that has the relief enamel jeweled effect of contemporary Sèvres combined with gold lizards from popular Japanese vases of the period.

The biscuit figures by Müller have natural appeal because they are essentially fine-looking. Each of the efforts from the Union Porcelain Works reveals an understanding of design and the medium, but the results are not easily admired today. The Union

88. Porcelain mug, Union Porcelain Works, 1882. *The Brooklyn Museum Collection.*

Porcelain Works output included handsome dinner-wares. The Smith family's own sets included one with handsome dark red borders and another with light green and gold. Dinnerware of those days had such curiously Victorian pieces as oyster plates with depressions molded in the shape of oyster shells.

The Trenton, New Jersey, potteries prospered after the Civil War. From concentrating on the more functional earthenwares in the 1850s there was a growth of interest in porcelain. Stephens, Tams, & Co., founded in 1861, had produced a stone china early in their career, but then made translucent china, and finally, as the Greenwood Pottery Co., produced an eggshell-thin, cream-colored body. This body, which was like the best Royal Worcester, was also made at Willets Manufacturing Company and the Ceramic Art Company in the 1880s. The outstanding Trenton Company of the time was Ott & Brewer, originally Bloor, Ott and Booth, and founded in 1863. The company had made high-fired earthenware for some time before it began producing porcelain in about 1876. At that time, with the aid of a sculptor, Isaac Broome, busts and groups were executed in Parian ware. A handsome bust of Cleopatra was made in two versions—in white and in polychrome. A vase celebrating baseball, with players on the base around a cone-shaped monument, was topped by an eagle. The work, logically, relates to the Union figures in that it reveals good craftsmanship and a sense of design burdened a little by an overstock of applied decorative themes.

Belleek is an extra-thin porcelain body that was perfected at Belleek, Ireland. It is a shiny, off-white body, which was made in a pottery that opened in 1857, but production there did not really get un-

89. Parian-ware bust of Ulysses S. Grant by Isaac Broome, Ott & Brewer, Trenton, New Jersey, 1875. *Collection of the Newark Museum.*

90. Parian-ware bust of George Washington, Ott & Brewer, Trenton, New Jersey, about 1876. *Collection of the Newark Museum.*

der way until 1863. On the American scene, a few pieces have turned up in Bennington which are thought to be early experiments of Belleek. The designs make them logical contemporaries of Irish experiments, but whether they are the result of attempting to glaze the Parian body without knowledge of the real Belleek, or are actually imitations of the Irish product, is not clear. Apparently the Bennington experiments were not put into production, and it was not until the 1880s that other potters seriously tried to create the characteristic body. In 1882, Ott & Brewer hired William Bromley of Belleek to assist them in their efforts to duplicate the body. This was achieved, and there are many delicate pieces of an extremely thin body from Ott

& Brewer. The work includes fine white pieces, such as a delicate tray with blue floral decoration.

The Midwest   Knowles, Taylor & Knowles, which had begun in East Liverpool, Ohio, in 1854 as a yellowware pottery operated by Isaac Knowles and Isaac Harvey, expanded gradually. By 1872 the firm was making a white graniteware. They were one of the largest American potters by 1900, producing hotel wares as one of their main items. Their interest in Belleek inspired them to lure Joshua Poole away from Belleek in 1887. The production of Belleek was undertaken for a brief time, but a fire in 1889 destroyed the china works. After that, their familiar variant, Lotus ware, was introduced, used for delicate pieces very close in spirit to Belleek. It was also used for more ambitiously decorated wares with jeweled details, openwork, and the cameo-like pâte-sur-pâte, best known in English examples by Minton. The Near East was a source of many forms for Knowles, Taylor & Knowles, but there was also a return to the classical in the colorfully decorated later Lotus ware.

Thin china, whether or not the body was identified as Belleek, was made by ambitious potters all over the country. Souvenir cups and saucers, vases, and other decorative pieces were made in Trenton and East Liverpool by smaller competitors of the companies mentioned. Also, potters in other areas, such as the Wheeling Pottery Company of Wheeling, West Virginia, produced handsome thin wares that were lavishly decorated.

Porcelain decorating was a significant field in the late nineteenth century, with New York a center for shops that were concerned with painting blanks, of both domestic and foreign origin. The decorating often was close to contemporary decorative mural

91. Part of a Belleek dessert set, Ott & Brewer, Trenton, New Jersey, about 1885. *Collection of the Newark Museum.*

92. Belleek cup and saucer, Willets Manufacturing Company, about 1890. *The Brooklyn Museum Collection.*

93. Belleek tray, Ott & Brewer, Trenton, New Jersey, about 1885. *The Brooklyn Museum Collection.*

94. Belleek vase, Ott & Brewer, Trenton, New Jersey, about 1890. *The Brooklyn Museum Collection.*

95. Lotus Ware ewer, a variation of Belleek, Knowles, Taylor & Knowles, East Liverpool, Ohio, about 1890. *The Brooklyn Museum Collection.*

96. Belleek dish, Ceramic Art Company, Trenton, New Jersey, about 1890. *The Brooklyn Museum Collection.*

97. Cameo Ware bowl, a variation of Belleek, Wheeling Pottery Company, Wheeling, West Virginia, about 1905. *The Brooklyn Museum Collection.*

98. Belleek pitcher by Walter Scott Lenox, Trenton, New Jersey, 1887. *The Brooklyn Museum Collection.*

99. Belleek basket by Walter Scott Lenox, Trenton, New Jersey, about 1900. *Collection of the Newark Museum.*

painting in following rococo models. Although much ambitious work was done in this field, the decoration of plates was frequently left to amateurs.

At the turn of the century, the more able manufacturers, such as the Ceramic Art Company, produced fine porcelains in designs that were rococo in spirit. When that company had changed its name to Lenox after 1900, its dinnerwares were made of a distinctive body in a modified neoclassical design.

Lenox and its numerous competitors produced wares in designs based on earlier styles that were freely adapted into so-called traditional styles. As at the beginning of the nineteenth century, porcelain design tended to be more conservative than earthenware design. Few American potters risked following such fads as art nouveau and modern art in porcelain.

CHAPTER VI

Art Pottery

Art pottery is a phenomenon of the nineteenth and twentieth centuries that offered a conscious answer to commercial decorative wares. While commercial designs were determined by popular demand and modified to meet the needs of quantity manufacturing, art pottery was, and still is, the domain of the artist-potter. For him ceramics are a medium of artistic expression to be executed by reviving the techniques individual craftsmen had used for centuries in creating an object from start to finish. Ceramics has special appeal to artists seeking a crafts medium because of the wide range of color and form clay affords.

The ideas that inspired art pottery were expressed in the writings of William Morris. He advocated reappraisals of the approaches to design and the techniques of producing decorative work. Morris' followers carried his thinking further and organized societies to promote artist-craftsmen about 1880 in what is called the Arts and Crafts Movement.

The Beginnings American art pottery's relationship to the Crafts Movement is a little confusing. In Cincinnati, Ohio, the origins of the most significant American art pottery can be traced to a china-painting course organized by Benn Pitman, an instructor at the Cincinnati School of Design in 1875. The group of ladies who learned how to decorate china met with

100. Earthenware tile by Trent Tile, Trenton, New Jersey, about 1885. *The Brooklyn Museum Collection.*

success and got more involved. Miss M. Louise McLaughlin was the outstanding member of the group. She developed her skills and was able to show her work at several large exhibitions, including the Exposition Universelle of 1879 in Paris, where she was awarded an honorable mention. The same year she started the Pottery Club.

The club met at the Dallas Pottery. Its members designed and decorated wares that were accurate reflections of the styles of the times. The Italian Renaissance, Hispano-Moresque, and oriental models inspired their efforts. Their work was high in quality, but there was insufficient financial support to continue after 1890.

Parallel to the Pottery Club was another group of ladies active at the same Dallas Pottery, although they were not members. Maria Longworth Nichols, their leader, found the Dallas Pottery inadequate because the kiln was constructed for high-fired wares and the heat was too great for underglaze colors. Her father sponsored the construction of a new pottery, the Rookwood Pottery, in 1880. The ladies worked with skilled craftsmen and able artists to produce a variety of wares. The output included a commercial ware made of a body similar to granite-ware, with an ivory finish. It consisted of dinner services and related household pieces decorated with underglaze blue and brown prints of birds, fishes, and other subjects from nature. The art wares that were offered were inspired by Japanese models. Decoration was most frequently light and in low relief on a dark, most often brown, ground. Beneath heavy, transparent-colored glazes there is a blending of rich tones of black, yellow, red, olive, green, and brown. There is an almost iridescent quality to highlights in light colors applied thickly over the ground. Before 1900 there was a certain amount of dull- or mat-finished ware made. Although it looks as though it has no glaze, it is easier to clean than biscuit wares because the surface is smoother. The forms and surfaces of Rookwood, beginning with oriental models, were predominantly subtle and

101. Earthenware vase, Rookwood Pottery, Cincinnati, Ohio, about 1900. *The Brooklyn Museum Collection.*

elongated. Active experimentation led to designs inspired by ancient Egyptian faience, and to broadening the ceramic bodies used. Whether consciously or not, art nouveau was the style in which much Rookwood was made. After 1889, Rookwood was a profitable venture, its products designed to appeal to many tastes. In 1893 its handsome display at the World's Columbian Exposition in Chicago included wares that suggest that Rookwood was more than an art pottery. The typical end-of-the-century classical forms with elaborate grotesques and other decoration were as much a part of things as the stylish art nouveau.

The popular Renaissance and Moorish themes were exploited by a number of potters after 1880. Another Cincinnatian, Matt Morgan, made ornate Moorish wares at his own establishment about 1900. Morgan's wares are decorative and in a popular rather than more serious vein of art pottery. He produced work that was purely decorative but was

102. Earthenware plate, Matt Morgan Art Pottery Company, Cincinnati, Ohio, about 1890. *The Brooklyn Museum Collection.*

not an expression of an artist involved in the aesthetic problems of his time. He is sometimes confused with William Morris' friend, the potter De Morgan, who was a serious designer and England's most important artist-potter, but Cincinnati was a far cry from London. Morgan was only one of a large group of men doing decorative work in the eclectic style. There are many more to be discovered, but standards must be applied. In spite of his shortcomings, Morgan was a fine craftsman and better than many other small manufacturers who did not understand the designs they adapted in haste.

Sophisticated Efforts in the Early Twentieth Century

Art nouveau had begun before 1900. Its elongated linear forms echoed the experiments of painters like Gauguin and Toulouse-Lautrec. The pale palette related to the popular academic painting of the time, also, and Rookwood was not the only pottery affected by it.

Artus van Briggle, who started at Rookwood and then had training as a painter in Paris, finally opened a pottery in Denver, Colorado, in 1899, where he specialized in art-nouveau forms in dull glazed wares close to the Egyptian influences in Rookwood. He even put the characteristic tall, thin girl of art-nouveau design inside a vase. More often he followed the safer models which go from art nouveau to art modern by squashing down the forms. The van Briggle factory never officially closed.

One constant source of difficulty in relating the history of American arts and crafts is that specific efforts invariably have failed because of finances; either they made money and became "commercial" or lost money and closed. Both Rookwood and van Briggle have been commercial in recent work. Having achieved reputations because their products were slanted toward fashionable innovations, they eliminated risk by being consistent.

More interesting but less spectacular—no lady painters (just customers) were involved—was the Chelsea Pottery. Alexander W. Robertson began it in 1866. By 1872, having been joined by his

103. Earthenware vase, Van Briggle Pottery Co., Colorado Springs, Colorado, about 1910. *The Brooklyn Museum Collection.*

father and brother, the firm was called James Robertson & Sons and began making decorative pieces. After 1875 they made a redware to imitate ancient Greek pottery, which was fine and yet was never popular. In 1877 they began making a glazed ware with floral decoration in relief. After 1884 there was a program of recreating the Chinese sang de boeuf. While this was well done, the limited edition of three hundred examples never sold out, and by 1889 the funds of Hugh Robertson, who had acquired control of the pottery, were exhausted. In 1891 he became manager of a reorganized Chelsea Pottery, which was soon making the crackleware for which it became famous. The pottery was moved from Chelsea, Massachusetts, to Dedham in 1896. Its most popular wares were crackled plates, bowls, mugs, cups, and saucers on which highly conventionalized natural forms were painted. Rabbit and

104. A collection of vases and bowls by Van Briggle Pottery Co., Colorado Springs, Colorado, 1900–10. *Robert and Gladys Koch, Norwalk, Connecticut.*

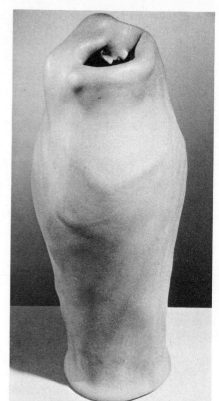

105. Earthenware vase, Van Briggle Pottery Co., Colorado Springs, Colorado, about 1900. *The Brooklyn Museum Collection.*

106. Bowl and plate with rabbit pattern, Dedham Pottery, Dedham, Massachusetts, 1910–30. *The Brooklyn Museum Collection.*

107. Biscuit-porcelain plaque, Chelsea Ceramic Art Works, Chelsea, Massachusetts, about 1880. *The Brooklyn Museum Collection.*

lion borders were most popular, but the swan, crab, iris, tulip, and other designs are also encountered. A popular version of the earlier experimental wares, volcanic ware, was another successful product at Dedham. It had the greatness of the early experiments, diluted in endless repetitions that were eminently more salable, although they contributed less to ceramic history than the sang de boeuf.

The Art Tile Works of John G. Low began operating in Chelsea in 1879. The characteristic tiles had designs in relief and colors in the palette appropriate to the moment—off-beat olives, mauves, gray-blues, yellow-browns, and the like. The tiles were sometimes decorated with portraits of famous men. Occasionally real leaves were pressed into the body to make a design. The Low tiles are similar to contemporary examples manufactured in Trenton in the late nineteenth century.

A number of small potters all over the country developed decorative lines that resembled those at Rookwood and Chelsea. There were efforts to capture the spirit of the more delicate porcelain wares that could be handled well (and best) by the biggest potteries.

More serious than most attempts were those of William H. Grueby, who set up the Grueby Faience Company in 1897 in South Boston. There they made architectural ceramics on a large scale, employing a hundred people. Because of this they were able to support the development of their artistic wares. The semi-porcelain (and quite hard) ceramic body employed was covered with a mat glaze. They made vases that are most easily described as freer versions of the mat-surfaced Rookwood. Tiles were a field of importance that has become familiar today. The decorated examples occasionally have mosaic pictures that are impressionistic in feeling. The crackleware they made was of high quality and is reminiscent of the oriental models which inspired it.

S. A. Weller of Zanesville, Ohio, was said to produce artwares as early as 1872. Best known are their twentieth-century work in art-nouveau shapes. Weller is identified by the iridescent qualities reminiscent of Tiffany glass.

By this point the reader will have discovered that there is an inconsistency in applying the term art pottery. It is occasionally used for the small group of artist-potters, but more often it is artistic wares for decoration that adhere more closely to fashion than do the products of larger potteries. In the nineteenth century the few potters who started out as serious artists either had to work in commercial potteries to make a living or disappeared.

At the turn of the century there were serious efforts at a few art schools to make pottery. These were significant because the men involved played an influential role at the time and made wares that were related to ideas current in architecture and painting. When these men made their livings

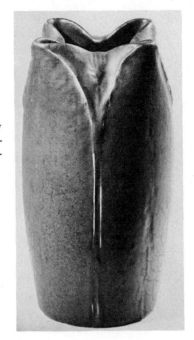

108. Earthenware vase, Grueby Faience Company, Boston, Massachusetts, about 1900. *The Brooklyn Museum Collection.*

109. Earthenware vase, S. A. Weller, Zanesville, Ohio, about 1905. *The Brooklyn Museum Collection.*

by teaching, they were able to continue making a serious contribution. Charles F. Binns, teaching at Alfred University from 1900 to 1931, was one of the foremost of these professor-potters, whose work reflects technical achievement and a profound understanding of pottery as an art. Another teacher, Arthur E. Baggs of Ohio State University, was a student of Binns. He was able to produce fine examples of the craft without attempting to be commercial or appealing. These two men are representative of a large group of able craftsmen who produced fine work while teaching. They mastered their craft and were close in spirit to the Japanese folk potters they respected. Working in simple forms and rough textures, they produced useful and handsome pieces. For collectors it is this field of pottery that might yield rich new material.

The stopping point for collecting ceramics is difficult to fix. It is safer to concentrate on earlier periods, for insight is gained as the gap between the maker and the viewer broadens. For practical reasons, it may be easier to make discoveries from the more recent times, but it is important to study collections and review known work in order to become the discoverer.

Index